PICKER'S
POCKET·GUIDE

TOYS

How to Pick Antiques like a Pro

ERIC BRADLEY

Published by

Krause Publications, a division of F+W, A Content + eCommerce Company
700 East State Street • Iola, WI 54990-0001
715-445-2214 • 888-457-2873
www.krausebooks.com

To order books or other products call toll-free 1-800-258-0929
or visit us online at www.krausebooks.com

On the cover: top row, from left: Buck Rogers Rocket Ship-see P. 145; a 1978 *Star Wars* R2-D2 figure, $190-$285 mint on card; Hot Wheels Deora vehicle, $400; **bottom row, from left**: Charlie Brown and Snoopy set-see P. 14; Winky Robot, circa 1950s, made by Tonezawa, Japan, 9-1/2" h, $635; see Model Trains, P. 158; Fisher Price toy with Doc & Dopey Dwarfs, 1938, each has a hammer that hits stump, red wheels, Model No. 770, $550-$1,600, depending on condition.

Back cover, top row from left: G.I. Joe Marine-see P. 117; Nintendo Game Boy-see P. 106; French doll-see P. 81; **bottom row, from left**: Steiff teddy bear-see P. 75; Superman badge-see P. 92; penny toy motorbike-see P. 56.

ISBN-13: 978-1-4402-4449-0
ISBN-10: 1-4402-4449-9

Designed by: Jana Tappa
Edited by: Kristine Manty

Printed in China

CONTENTS

Dedication

To my son, Patrick, a collector at heart who is always up for a flea market or a road trip.

Acknowledgments

Special thanks to: Stephen Lanzilla of the Boston Area Toy Collecting Club; Kevin Stark for designing my favorite toys from childhood and for the private tour of the Toy & Action Figure Museum; Keith Moniz for sharing his picking tips; Steve Siemens of Toybase 10; David Kaelin and Michael Thomasson for sharing their passion for vintage video games; David Pressland and Michael Bertoia for their wisdom on tin toys; Hot Wheels expert Michael Zarnock; Brian Listman of Christmas 1970; Doug Kale and the vendors at the North Dallas Toy Show; Anthony Bearden for making a life selling vintage LEGO sets; and the late Donald Kaufman for sharing his passion with me during his last days on Earth.

Many thanks are owed to Jack Kelly for his wonderful photos of collectors in action. Deep thanks to the various auction houses and dealers (listed in the Resources Section) for images from past auctions, particularly Alex Winter and the staff at Hake's Americana & Collectibles; the staff at Morphy Auctions; Joalien Johnson and Leigh Gotch at Bonhams and William Morford at Wm. Morford Auctions.

Introduction

You are a toy collector.

It was your first collection. Your parents and family likely started your collection months before you were even born. With every birthday party and holiday, your collection grew and grew. Remember running across a department store to see what new finds were worthy of your toy box? What about building a spaceship from an empty box or a figure from a scrap of wood? Me, too. That's because no other hobby touches every single person in the world quite like toys.

The people who collect vintage toys are those who are simply revisiting their first collection. In some cases, they never left it. That's the thing about toy collecting: You can find amazing examples in abundant supply from any time period – especially your own. Vintage toys radiate a certain aura, energy, if you will, that instantly conveys the zeitgeist of the era it was made.

Mega collector Martin Parr, in his attempt to explain his eclectic collection, sums this up when he writes, "I am very attracted to objects which are ephemeral. Their significance and cultural context changes as the world moves on. Many of these objects are associated with people or events that are bound up with the glories of a certain time and place. When these glories fade, the object takes on a certain resonance."

Sales data shows you'll have lots of company in your toy collecting hobby, but also lots of competition for finer examples. The collectible toy business is one of the largest in both the retail market and the secondary market and is also perhaps one of the first types of established collecting genres ever defined. It's interesting to note that FAO Schwarz, founded in 1862 as America's first toy store, launched its "Toy Bazaar" antique toy department in the early 1960s to meet collector demand. Toy collecting is an old and venerated hobby.

No figures are kept for the number of vintage collectible toys sold every year, but the number sold at auction is growing. At any given time, more than 5 million toys are for sale or taking bids on eBay. LiveAuctioneers, one of the world's largest auctions-hosting websites, shows an estimated half million toys were sold by brick and mortar auction houses at auction

Toys are the No. 1 collectible category across all age groups and it's no wonder. The toys that fascinated us, kept us safe, and filled our childhood with fun look all the more appealing as we grow older.
Courtesy of Jack Kelly

during the last 16 years. In many cases, these sales have set new records as collections finally come to market after decades in private hands.

Among these private collections, few reached the size, scope, and value of that owned by Donald Kaufman. His family founded Kay Bee Toys in 1922 and at one point the Kaufmans operated 605 stores in 44 U.S. states, Puerto Rico, and Guam. The company's world headquarters was based in Pittsfield, Mass., just about an hour east of Brimfield, Mass., home to America's largest outdoor flea market and antiques show. It was a perfect opportunity for Donald. His love of toys and pop culture was backed by his fascination with clockwork and pressed tin automotive toys. For more than 40 years, he haunted the shows at Brimfield, traded with collectors, and was a familiar face at toy auctions and shows up and down the east coast. At best count, the collection totaled 7,000 toys with no duplicates — the collection had the finest example of every important antique transportation toy ever made.

In a strange twist, Kaufman both embraced the social aspect of collecting yet never told anyone about the collection's size and scope — even his children didn't see it. Only about 20 people ever saw the collection in its entirety. He kept it securely stored and on private display in a dedicated wing off his home. Donald granted only two interviews before he died: one to *The New York Times* and one to me.

"I always thought: 'This is what I want to do,'" he told me, just weeks before he passed away in 2009. "I want to build this building and fill it up with toys and make it so that I can fit as many toys in there as I have to get. Other people would say, 'Oh, I don't have room.' Well, I always had room. There was always room for one more toy and I could always figure out how to put up another shelf."

When he announced in 2009 that he was going to sell his collection, the news wasn't much of a surprise to the hobby. But when his fellow collectors learned of its quality and completeness, it was a stunner. When they also learned he was ill and would likely not live to see the final auction of his amazing toys, the outpouring of support was immense. Donald felt collectors would care for the toys better than any museum ever could: "I'm going to sell it back to the collectors who are going to take care of them. They are going to be their prized possessions."

American National fire pumper pedal car, all original form with upright boiler and wood side ladders, ex, 60" l, **$10,350**. Donald Kaufman Collection.

Courtesy of Bertoia Auctions

It took four auctions to sell the great Kaufman collection of automotive toys for a record $12.1 million. The collection stands as the most valuable of its kind in the history of the world.

You don't need to spend $12 million on toys to have an amazing collection. But it certainly helps to bring a fraction of the passion Donald brought to his hobby. You probably have a few toys hanging around the house and it's never been easier to find unusual examples. Adding to them can turn addictive, especially when you find ones you had as a kid … or the ones you always wanted.

The public's love affair with toys both vintage and contemporary shows no signs of slowing down. With more than 74.3 million children in the United States alone, according to ChildStats.gov, toys are big business. The U.S. domestic market for retail toys hit $22.09 billion in 2013, according to the Toy Industry Association. Compared to the $635 million sold at the height of the Baby Boomer Generation in 1960, that's a mind-boggling 3,364 percent increase. That's amazing considering the total number of children has only grown by 13 percent.

IN THIS BOOK

From Cracker Jack to the Xbox, toys speak volumes about our culture, our past times, and our collections. This book will

During the last decade, LEGO has transcended its origins as a toy brick company to a pinnacle of licensing. The LEGO *Star Wars* line of toys is one of the most collectible in the last 50 years, resulting in seven-figure auction values for rare sets. This set of three droid LEGO figures are valued at a combined **$25** by collectors. *Courtesy of Eric Bradley*

show you where to find vintage toys and how to buy and sell to become a true collector of great toys. Condition is the chief factor in collecting toys and this book aims to depict top examples from several different collecting categories. It will also touch on the history of select categories, look at common fakes and reproductions and give you a working vocabulary to speak and think intelligently about this exciting and varied collecting field.

As you read the book, pay special attention to the "Picker's Tip" boxes distributed across its chapters. Together, we'll look at why toys have influenced the world's most valuable fine art and understand how vintage toys have come to dominate the antiques collecting landscape. We'll also learn how these trends have affected fair market values. There are no rules on what toys to collect but there are criteria all valuable collections have in common: Condition, Authenticity, Provenance, Exposure and Quality. Combined, we'll learn how to focus on the most popular collecting genres and target the most valuable examples in each. You may be pleasantly surprised to see the diversity of the chapters in this book. A lot has changed in the toy collecting hobby during the last 15 years or so and this book aims to give a "500-foot view" of the hobby's latest collecting areas.

You'll also hear from toy collectors themselves, as well as auctioneers who specialize in vintage and antique toys. Playing a leading role in one of the hottest collecting categories in the

Bring back some memories? Collectors even seek out vintage catalogs stocked with images of toys. This set of four sold for **$163** in July 2014. See more about these repositories of research in Chapter 1.

Courtesy of Hakes Americana & Collectibles

hobby, they have dozens of tips to share to help you become a more intelligent collector and picker.

Hopefully, you'll look at your own collection in a new light or, at the very least, become inspired to start a new collection. Nothing else quite kindles our nostalgia for our beloved childhood — or of simpler times gone by — like our favorite toy. Who doesn't remember curling up with the annual *Sears Wish Book* or circling photos in the FAO Schwarz catalog? As always, I hope all of this inspires you to get out and about, make new friendships, and start a fresh hunt for some of the most wondrous collectibles ever made.

A NOTE ABOUT VALUES

The values you see in this book are prices realized at public auction. They are a snapshot based on certain conditions of sale that were met on the day they were offered for auction. Values will change based on many factors. For more detailed market analysis, I encourage you to visit the bibliography to find books dedicated to certain collecting categories.

Popeye Menu Free Ball Game, 1935, Durable Toy and Novelty Corp., tin litho with metal pegs and marbles, from the Don Vernon Collection, very good condition, 14" x 23", **$75-$200** depending on condition. *Courtesy of Heritage Auctions*

James Bond 007 Thunderball Special Agent Rifle, circa 1965, Tada, Japan, for distribution by Lone Star, England, in original box, plastic, battery–operated rifle with a removable dart pistol hidden inside front grip; rarest of all Bond toy guns (this example originally came out of a Japanese toy museum), near mint, rare, box: 25" x 8", rifle: 23" l, **$2,400**. *Courtesy of Morphy Auctions*

Home Run King Mechanical Game, late 1930s, Selrite Products, Inc. of New York, tin wind-up, "hopper" filled with small baseballs as mechanism lifts one ball up for the batter to swing and knock the ball off the tee, very good, **$900-$1,200**. *Courtesy of Heritage Auctions*

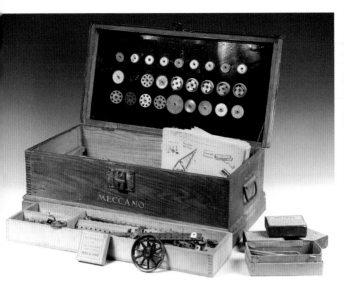

One of the most successful toy lines in history, Meccano Mechanical Toys set the stage for TinkerToys and LEGO popular today. This set in an original oak chest with decal, circa 1916, has nickel-plated structural components, solid brass gears, black painted cast wheels, four boxes of nuts and bolts, chains, etc, plus clockwork Motor No 2. The set was made in Wurttemberg, Germany, measures 8" x 11" x 22" and has its original instruction booklet, **$250**.

Courtesy of Thomaston Place Auctions

During the 1890s, the Ives Manufacturing Co. was in its prime producing masterpieces in cast iron detail. In 2014, this Ives cutter sleigh with walking horse sold for **$238,450**. *Courtesy of Bertoia Auctions*

This set of *Peanuts* characters includes a soft rubber "squeaker" toy version of Snoopy with a long nose, dated 1958, standing approximately 7-1/2" h; and a harder rubber version of Charlie Brown from the 1960s (no specific date listed), 9" h, fine, **$95**.

Courtesy of Heritage Auctions

CHAPTER 1

Top Collectible Toys By Decade

The toy business and the toy collecting hobby are surviving in the midst of genre-busting trends.

The arrival of the internet made it cheaper and easier for collectors to buy, sell and trade, and share information than ever before. Now the mobile revolution — ushered in with smartphones and tablets — are driving demand for digitally-interactive toys.

Demand is also changing as more and more segments of the global population finally reach the affluence level attained by the United States in the 20th century. Economies in Brazil, Russia, India, and China are producing a middle class faster than America did between 1945-1985. Global wealth is expected to top more than $345 trillion by 2016, a three-fold increase from 2000.[1] It's too early to tell if these newly minted consumers will fall in love with vintage American toys the way we did during this time.

This list is not intended to include every popular toy offered during this period. In some cases, the most popular toys sold at least 10 million copies and enough examples exist to satisfy collector demand and keep demand relatively stable.[2] While a history of toys could fill an entire library, these are a few of the hotly collected toys from years past. Each decade brought new innovations — and one-hit wonders — that once stole our hearts and now dominate toy auctions.

1825-1880s

The Industrial Revolution allowed the large-scale mechanization of toy manufacturing in both America and Europe. This

---

1 Credit Suisse Global Wealth Report, 2011.
2 If you want this, check out Tim Walsh's magnum opus, *The Playmakers*, aka *Timeless Toys*.

period is deemed by experts as the "Golden Age" of American tin toy manufacturing and it produced dazzling metal toys, the likes of which the public has never seen since. As the earliest American toy factory on record, Francis, Field and Francis (aka the Philadelphia Tin Toy Manufactory) opened a tin plate kitchenware factory on South Market Street in Philadelphia in 1838. By the early 1840s, it had expanded into toys such as tin and iron wagons and floor trains. George W. Brown and Co. produced the first American clockwork toys in 1856. America's oldest toy shop, FAO Schwarz, opened in 1862. By the 1860s-1880s, production was extensive in factories of Althof Bergmann and Co., Hull and Stafford, James Fallows, Edward Ives, Merriam Manufacturing Co. and Stevens and Brown.[3] Toys from these makers are the most sought after by collectors and routinely bring four to five figures at auction. Unfortunately, not much is known about the early history of these firms.

1890s

Cast iron toys dominated the international market during the 1890s and dozens of toy makers sparked intense competition, partially fuelled by the Sears, Roebuck and Co. catalog, which reached more rural communities in the later part of the decade. Companies such as J. & E. Stevens Co. introduced fanciful designs and dramatic visuals. In Europe, the Märklin company (Gebr. Märklin & Cie. GmbH) had already perfected the tin toy and introduced its first wind-up toy train in 1891. American firms, such as Pratt & Letchworth, specialized in cast iron toys that were miniature versions of real life, horse-drawn hook and ladder trucks or sulkys. The R. Bliss Manufacturing Co., initially produced piano cabinet parts, developed some of the finest cardboard and paper lithographed toys ever made. The Wilkins Toy Company was founded in 1890 on sheet metal toys, but was purchased in 1894 by Harry T. Kingsbury, who would go on to found Kingsbury, a famous American cast iron toy company. The Ives Manufacturing Co. was in its prime at this time and producing masterpieces in cast iron detail. In 2014, an Ives cutter sleigh with walking horse sold for $238,450.

---

3 One paragraph does not give this important period justice. Thankfully, *Art of the Tin Toy*, by David Pressland, covers it in depth. If you are interested in collecting or trading toys from this period, his book is a must-own body of research.

Battleship Toy Blocks, circa 1890s, boxed set, large paper covered wooden toy puzzle blocks by McLoughlin Bros., NY, to form different beautifully lithographed images of US Naval White Squadron ships, excellent, 11-1/8" x 21-1/8" x 2-7/8", **$345**.

Courtesy of William Morford Investment Grade Collectibles at Auction

1900s

The Edwardian Era delivered a great diversity of metal toys collectors pursue today, including penny toys and cast iron masterpieces. German toymaker Ernst Paul Lehmann Patenwerk had been active since 1880, but the early 1900s saw his most popular innovations with lithographed and hand-painted tin. His shop in Brandenberg, Germany, perfected the clockwork tin toy and Lehmann toys bring as much as $13,000 at auction. Ferdinand Strauss also created exceptional tin litho wind-up toys, as did Friedrich Adolf Richter. A group of fans refounded Richter's factory in 1993 and are reproducing his famous stone construction toy sets. Gunthermenn hit its stride in this decade as well and its mechanical toy cars are hot, as are its elaborate mechanical toys, which are in major collections around the world. The craftsmanship of the tin and mechanical toys of this period are especially impressive. Perhaps the most sought after toy born during this decade was the Lionel train, which you can learn about in detail in Chapter 10.

1910s

This era saw the debut of popular culture personalities appear in toy form. Comic strip characters such as Happy Hooligan and Foxy Grandpa showed up in cast iron nodder form from

Kenton Hardware Co. Early wind-up figures of Charlie Chaplin's Little Tramp character sell for up to $1,000. Affordable baseball-themed games appeared during this decade and toy soldiers were also popular toys at the time. This decade also gave us Erector sets thanks to Alfred Carlton Gilbert and his Mysto Manufacturing Co. Complete sets from the 1920s-30s bring as much as $17,000 at auction.

1920s

The 1920s saw the Hubley Company hit its stride and its cast iron Monkey Cage Wagon now brings as much as $95,000 at auction. As automobiles became more common place, the arrival of quality vehicle toys dominated this decade. The Moline Pressed Steel Co. started making Buddy "L" toys in 1921 and its all-steel miniature trucks and farm implement toys can sell for as much as $5,000 in top condition. A popular toy in many collections is the Marx Merrymakers, a late 1920s wind-up toy that can sell for $3,000+. Character toys featured radio (Amos & Andy) and comic strip characters (Smitty) from Famous Artists Syndicate and these toys have tremendous crossover appeal. A weird standout from this decade is the 8-inch long Hi-Way Henry Tin Toy Automobile. Inventor Oscar Hitt claimed the elaborate toy was based on a comic strip of his own design, yet no example of the strip or characters has ever been found. Made by Fischer, the toy now brings as much as $4,000 at auction (the toy was reproduced in 1980 and retailed for $800). This decade also saw Japanese mak-

Kitchen playsets were big sellers during the 1920s and this unusual, early boxed set of "Play House Kitchen Room" includes metal kitchen toy furniture pieces (stove, hoosier cabinet, sink and pantry cabinet) in great paint, by Henry Katz Toys, in as found in excellent never used condition, box size: 11-3/4" x 11" x 3-1/2", **$467**.

Courtesy of William Morford Investment Grade Collectibles at Auction

ers begin large-scale exports; Japanese toy makers of this era — late 1920s and early 1930s — used very bright, unusual colors. By 1927, All Metal Products Co. making toys under the Wyandotte brand name became the largest makers of toy guns in the U.S. — a distinction the firm held for decades.

1930s

You'd think the decade that saw the Great Depression would also see a dearth of neat toys, but it appears the opposite is true. The 1930s ushered in an explosion of productivity by the Marx company, including Buck Rogers space toys. Mickey Mouse toys

Lone Ranger/Midway Two-Sided Target Practice Game Board, Louis Marx, 1938. See additional photo and information on P. 20.
Courtesy of Heritage Auctions

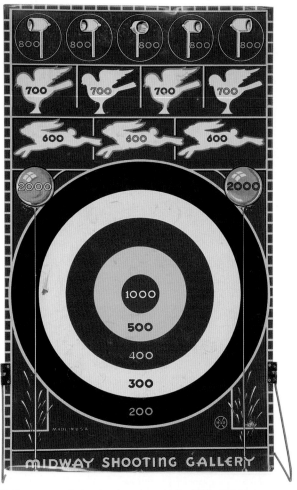

Radio stars were featured on lots of toys in the 1930s. This Lone Ranger tin over cardboard target practice board was designed to be used with rubber tipped suction-cup spring loaded dart toy gun and was offered with its original box, 6" w x 27" h, **$42**.

Courtesy of Heritage Auctions

hit the marketplace with a bang and a famous Tipp & Co. tin litho motorcycle featuring Mickey and Minnie sold at auction for $47,500 in 2013. More comic and cartoon characters were licensed for toys and Popeye and Betty Boop first appeared in tin and celluloid form for the first time. The *Sears Wish Book*, known as the *Sears Christmas Book* catalog, debuted in 1933, and became a cultural touchstone.

1940s

The first Superman toys hit the market in the early 1940s, and a 13-inch wood and composition jointed Ideal Novelty and Toy Co. Superman figure, which originally sold for 94 cents, now sells northward of $800 in fine condition. This decade really belongs to the Walt Disney Co., which saw exponential growth on the gains it made in the 1930s with Pinocchio, Goofy, Bambi, Dumbo, Three Little Pigs, and Donald Duck all appearing on desirable toys. Early Bugs Bunny toys appeared in the 1940s, too, as 34-inch tall felt figures by the M&H Novelty Co. World War II affected the toy market deeply as toy companies were quickly called on to convert machinery for the war effort. Scrap drives for metal and paper claimed countless historical toys as school

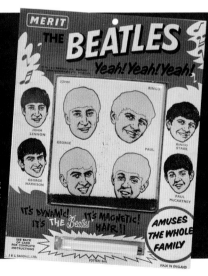

Celebrities inspired a slew of toys and games to capitalize on their fame, such as this Beatles Magnetic Hair Game Complete with Wand by Merit (UK NEMS, 1964). This heavyweight card with hairless images of The Beatles has a hard plastic cover full of black magnetic shavings that can be moved into place using the included "magnetic pencil," 8" x 10-1/2", **$600-$700.**

Courtesy of Heritage Auctions

groups on both sides of the Atlantic specifically encouraged children. This is one reason why pre-war toys with original paper boxes are so highly treasured now. As quickly as possible, toy manufacturing resumed in the mid-1940s, but that only meant America now faced competition from Japanese companies. The J. Chein & Co., known for tin litho mechanical toys, struggled at this time but found salvation with the F.W. Woolworth Company. A second challenge facing Chein was the introduction of plastic toys in the late 1940s.

Scrap drives for metal and paper claimed countless historical toys as school groups on both sides of the Atlantic specifically encouraged children. This British boy gladly gives up his tin litho airplane to a soldier in this propaganda photo shot during World War II.

Photo courtesy Library of Congress Prints and Photographs Division; Toni Frissell, 1945, photographer.

1950s

Plastics revolutionized the toy industry in a way not seen since the Industrial Revolution. Cheaper to produce and ship, the toys broke far more easily than their tin and cast iron counterparts. However, it was easier to incorporate electronics into plastic toys, a development that ushered in an era of space toys. Early electric and battery-operated toys from the 1950s are in high demand now: tinplate robots by Modern Toys of Japan, Japanese boats by K&O Models, electric vehicles made by the Urbana Mfg. Co. in Ohio. The 1950s also marked an explosion of Japanese toy makers, such as Yonezawa, whose space toys can bring as much as $20,000, and Cadillac friction cars bring more than $1,000+ at auction. PEZ toy dispensers finally reached the United States in 1957 after being introduced in 1927 in Austria.

1960s

The 1960s sparked several social revolutions and the toy market was no exception. With Barbie's debut in 1959, the 1960s were dominated by a fashion doll revolution. A G.I. Joe prototype appearing in 1964 (later selling for $200,001 in 2003) sparked the action figure revolution. By 1965, Rock 'em Sock 'em Robots

The emotional and psychological bond children have with their toys cannot be overstated. Here, an abandoned boy holds a stuffed toy animal amid the ruins following German aerial bombing of London in 1945. Besides the clothes on his back, the toy elephant is likely his only worldly possession.

Photo courtesy Library of Congress Prints and Photographs Division; Toni Frissell, 1945, photographer.

appeared and collectors are now willing to pay up to $300 for a Marx set in its original box. Remote control toys were perfected around this time and collectors are now paying up to $750 for examples in original boxes, such as the Tiger Joe Tank made by DeLuxe and more than $1,500 for a battery-operated "Franken-stein" Toy by Marx. Spanning the late 1950s to the early 1960s, the Masudaya "Gang of Five" toy robots used remote controls to operate the tin litho creations that now fetch more than $45,000 at auction. Highly detailed battery toys distributed by Cragstan during the 1960s are prized now; the company distributed toys produced by Nomura, Masudaya, Yoshiya, Daiya, Horikawa and Yonezawa but some Cragstan toys are found for as low as $20 to $30 online. LEGO building sets hit the U.S. market in 1961 after appearing overseas in 1953. Batman toys from the 1960s "Batma-nia" craze are still bringing good prices.

Fleagle, Bingo, Drooper, and Snorky were the main characters of the 1960s Saturday morning television program, *The Banana Splits*. The plush character toys stand roughly 9" to 12" h and are valued at about **$10-20 each**. *Courtesy of Heritage Auctions*

1970s

Leading collectible toys include MEGO action figures and playset lines related to popular feature films and television series such as *Planet of the Apes* and *Space 1999*. Technically debut-ing in 1968, Hot Wheels dominated the 1970s, as did other cast vehicle lines such as Dinky, Corgi, and Matchbox. One of the most famous Hot Wheels sets was the 1970 Mongoose & Snake Drag Race Set, which now trades for between $300 and $400. A complete collection of 1968-1972 Hot Wheels Redlines sold for $4,300 at auction in 2011 and a 1970 Hot Wheels store display with 12 original cars sold for $3,000 in 2012. The J. Chein & Co. ceased all toy production in 1979.

1980s

Now considered officially vintage, the most sought after toys from the 1980s are often in mint condition and still in their original boxes. A slew of toys were reproduced or "reissued" during the 1980s, most notably the tin Amos & Andy clockwork toy vehicle, a line of metal toys by Paya (970 Bugatti), and a line of Steiff teddy bears.[4] The amount of reproductions and reissues that appeared during the 1980s cannot be overstated and if you find a vintage toy that looks just too good to be true, it could be from the 1980s. A Voltron I AFA 85 robot brought $550 in 2012. Unusual limited edition toys are seeing strong prices recently with collector's edition teddy bears and Les-Paul collector trucks selling for more than $200. Leading this decade is the plethora of *Star Wars* action figures, vehicles, and play sets; groups of 30 figures can bring more than $1,000 in online auctions. A distant second is mint-condition toys from the *He-Man and the Masters of the Universe* series with Eternia playsets bringing $700. The fledgling market for vintage video games is growing with some games bringing good money as described in chapter 12. The 3-1/2-inch line of G.I. Joe action figures were introduced in the 1980s, but secondary market prices have not met those set by their 1960s counterparts.

1990s

Japanese tin windup toys reproduced in the 1990s are often sold as original. World renowned expert Mark Chervenka says the key to recognizing the Kitahara copies is Kitahara's own trademark on the 1990s copies. The Kitahara mark is a crown enclosing the initials "TK" surrounded by a banner with the word "Toy." A popular line of "vintage-inspired" space toys were produced at this time, but these contemporary, limited edition collector's items can sell for as much as $900 at auction. Disney toys sold by Schylling can be confused as vintage despite being mass produced in China. Some early figures based on the Disney Pixar film *Toy Story* are bringing as much as $70 at auction. WWF Superstars Wrestling Action figures can sell for $30-$40 each, if mint on card. Groups of toys and accessories from the Littlest Pet Shop are starting to appear at auction with prices ranging between $80 and $125, depending on the number of pieces.

---

4 RealorRepro.com (powered by RubyLane.com) lists many of these toys.

BLACK AMERICANA TOYS

Despite their often derogatory nature, Black Americana toys remain so popular with collectors that many are reproduced. There is no doubt these toys perpetuated racial stereotypes on retailer's shelves from the 1860s well into the 1950s. Themes of many black toys were based solely on caricatures, especially The Golliwog (or Golliwogg), which was a popular children's book character in England beginning in the 1890s. Among the more famous black toys is "Dancing Sam," originally a wooden figure held by a stick. Contemporary handmade toys are eagerly collected as folk art, rather than as a toy. Contemporary toy companies such as HIA Toys, Uzuri Kid Kidz, and EthiDolls, embrace multiculturalism and present positive images of historical leaders and children.

Early tin litho dancing mechanical black jazz musician toy (squeezing lever on back makes his arms, legs, eyes and mouth move, cymbals clash, etc.), excellent, 6-1/2" h x 2-1/4" w x 1" d, **$316**.

Courtesy of William Morford Investment Grade Collectibles at Auction

Tombo the Alabama Coon Jigger Mechanical Wind-up Toy, Ferdinand Strauss, patent date May 24, 1910, 9-3/4" h when assembled, **$700-$800**.

Courtesy of Heritage Auctions

Sambo Metal Target Board, All Metal Products Co., 1930s, colorful meal cover over cardboard backing accompanied by original cardboard box, excellent, **$119**.

Courtesy of Heritage Auctions

"Big Time Marionette," 1930s, Hull Manufacturing Co. of Hagerstown, MD, painted pressed composition head, fabric clothing, stiff cardboard interior and wooden feet with original cardboard marionette handle attached with original strings, lid end panel is marked "Rastus," a politically incorrect pejorative term traditionally associated with African Americans that is considered offensive; good condition; marionette: 12-1/2" h, box: 6" w x 9" h x 2" d, **$115**.

Courtesy of Hakes Americana & Collectibles

Patriotic Drum, very early, high quality toy drum, detailed designs on wood bands at top and bottom; with embossed lithographed American flag images in metal all around the sides, excellent, 6-3/4" x 9" dia, **$467**.

Courtesy of William Morford Investment Grade Collectibles at Auction

One of the many side projects the famous Lionel model train company pursued attempted to open sales to the little girls of the period. This green and cream porcelain stove on steel legs featured two working burners and an oven. Emblazoned with the Lionel logo on the back panel and a temperature gauge on the front of the oven door this working stove must have been a great joy for the aspiring bakers of the 1940s. It is understood that Lionel manufactured this stove for only one year in 1932 and ceased production

due to poor sales resulting from the Great Depression; as such, these stoves are somewhat hard to come by, 25-1/2" w x 33" h x 11-1/2" d, **$266**. *Courtesy of James D. Julia Auctioneers, Fairfield, Maine, www.jamesdjulia.com*

With raw materials scarce, many war-time toy makers shifted into smaller items. This collection of toys from the World War I era includes a boxed Magic Cork game, Vanishing Handkerchief, trick card games, multiple hand tricks with miniature billiard balls, various dexterity puzzles, the Mysto Phantom Card Trick in original package, a novelty toy of a WWI tin tank, steamboat playing cards, and more. The set sold for **$151**.

Courtesy of James D. Julia Auctioneers, Fairfield, Maine, www.jamesdjulia.com

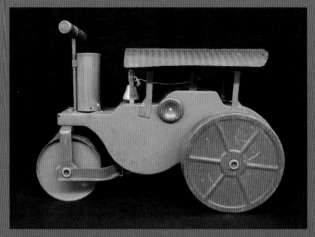

World War II had a profound effect on the global toy business. Before the war, the Keystone Co. of New England factory produced toys and kiddie rides, such as this steam roller. After converting its machinery, it produced radio filter boxes for tanks and jeeps. The small parts shown in the picture are used in the filter boxes. A pre-war Keystone Steam Roller 60, as seen in the image, is now sold for as much as **$300** at auction.

Keystone Steam Roller 60 Toy Factory Conversion: Howard Hollem, Photographer,
Farm Security Administration - Office of War Information Photograph Collection
(Library of Congress); Keystone Steamroller-1 & 2: Paige Auction

Toy playsets crossed the line between dress-up and toys. In this period photo taken in Macy's New York toy department, Alex Mumford Jr., 10, is disguised as the Man From U.N.C.L.E., complete with eye patch, handcuffs, trench coat, knife, gun, and briefcase. Alex would have to pay $200-$300 today to own the Man From U.N.C.L.E. Spy Attache Case Toy (Ideal, 1965) he played with as a kid. The original includes a case, including the gun, clip, and dart; cigarette lighter/case with hidden gun and controls, several badges, and cards.

Alex Mumford Jr., Man from U.N.C.L.E.: *Courtesy Library of Congress Prints and Photographs Division;* Man From U.N.C.L.E. Spy Attache Case Toy (Ideal, 1965), **$200-$300**: *Courtesy of Heritage Auctions.*

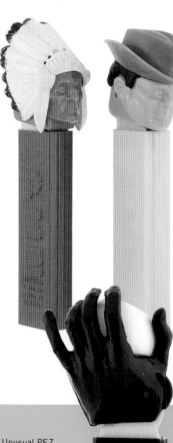

PEZ toy dispensers finally reached the United States in 1957 after being introduced in 1927 in Austria. The company is still producing new toys thanks to marketing agreements with Disney and *Star Wars*. This PEZ Indian Chief and Cowboy set is marked "Made In Austria" and dates to the early 1970s, 4-1/2" h pair, **$158**.

Courtesy of Hake's Americana & Collectibles

Unusual PEZ with green pupil eyeball in hand which is black variety, circa late 1960s, these were issued with one of four different stickers, either on one or both sides, this is one-sticker variety which has "LUV PEZ" on side, very fine, 4-1/4" h, **$216**.

Courtesy of Hake's Americana & Collectibles

Display model dolls, Mickey & Minnie Mouse, circa 1931, designed by doll maker Charlotte Clark, produced in very limited quantities for the sole purpose of promotion via the most prominent movie theaters and retail stores. Stuffed velveteen, Minnie has hundreds of individual eyelashes, each has a long, 32" tail, near mint, rare, Mickey: 44" to the tips of ears; Minnie: 48" to top of flower, **$151,534.** *Courtesy of Hakes Americana & Collectibles*

CHAPTER 2

Recent Values

Toy collecting allows for an infinite number of specialized collecting variations. Want cast iron cars made between 1930 and 1940? You could start with the Hubley Manufacturing Co. and collect by size. Only want dolls that were first introduced as paper dolls in the early 1950s? Betsy McCall is your gal. Have an affinity for pre-war metal squirt guns made in Michigan? Versions made by All Metal Products Co., better known as Wyandotte Toys, can be found for $20 on up, depending on condition. With toys, your collection can be as specialized or as general as you want it to be.

TODAY'S TREND: THE BEST OR NOTHING

Much like other collecting categories, serious collectors open their wallets wide for rare and unusual antique toys. In 2007, auctioneer Ted Hake shattered existing auction records for a Walt Disney toy when he sold a pair of rare, giant display-model dolls of Mickey Mouse and Minnie Mouse for $151,534. This after the seller originally posted them on eBay for a mere $50,000 with no luck. The dolls were made circa 1930-31 in very limited quantities for the sole purpose of promotion via the most prominent movie theaters, retail stores, and even the occasional photo shoot with Walt himself. Designed by master toy designer Charlotte Clark, the Mickey stands an astounding 44 inches to the tips of his ears; Minnie is 48 inches to the top of her flower.

The dolls were in immaculate condition for their age and were described as "near-mint." To this day, Ted still considers the pair the best thing he's ever auctioned. When bidding opened, the pair was presented with an estimate of $20,000 to $35,000, no doubt because of the lack of interest when they appeared on eBay for $50,000. But to an advanced collector, the estimate did not matter. Here was an opportunity to own what experts at the time considered the only known existing set in drop dead mint condition. Those facts — combined with Hake's sterling reputation as an honest and knowledgeable auctioneer — meant competition would be fierce to own the set. When the auction closed at 4:37 p.m. on Sept. 27, 2007, the lot set a record for a Disney doll sold at auction that has yet to be beat nearly nine years later.

When non-collectors hear about a sale such as the Charlotte Clark Mickey Mouse dolls, the response can be outright incredulity. But it's not so difficult to understand those headline-grabbing prices if you look at the toy under the same criteria used to evaluate fine art or even luxury real estate. Toy values are chiefly influenced by demand, rarity, and condition. But there are other factors as well. Michael Findlay in his book, *The*

Toy shows are an excellent source for small toys priced under $100 thanks to specialty dealers, who often find it easier to sell in person than consigning to an auction. *Courtesy of Jack Kelly*

Value of Art, lays down five main criteria pertaining to fine art that are also useful for explaining why some toy values set and hold records for years. The world's most valuable toys have the following five things in common: Authenticity, Exposure, Provenance, Quality, and, most importantly, Condition.

Authenticity is black or white. There are no gray areas with Authenticity: Either the toy is right or it is wrong. It is either authentic or it is a fake.

Exposure influences demand for a work and brings prestige to its owner. When Steve Geppi, the president and CEO of Diamond Comic Distributors, paid $200,000 for the world's most valuable action figure — the first handcrafted prototype of the 1963 G.I. JOE® action figure (see P. 122) — the sale made international news and earned a Guinness World Record. "My purchase of G.I. Joe does not mean that he will go into a dark and dusty bank vault," Geppi said at the time. "I plan on making sure he is visible ... In addition to having him displayed ... I also plan to lend him as a fund raising attraction to veterans groups and other related charities."

Vintage Toy Cap Gun Group, 1950s: Three vintage toy pistols, including two Cowboy-type cap guns, and one small Dick Tracy-style (has "Dick" embossed on handle sides) pistol. The set of three sold for **$74**. *Courtesy of Heritage Auctions*

Exposure is crucial for building collector demand around a single piece or an entire category. Exposure also often improves our collective education about the toy's designer, manufacturer, and place in culture. Tom Khayos, a toy reviewer and action figure collector who authors a pop culture blog titled, "Raging Nerdgasm," says exposure can instantly impact a figure's value in a matter of hours. "The toy field is a liquid market," he says, "which means the price is often dependent on current demand for the product. Someone may not think their Bucky O'Hare figures are worth anything, but something as simple as a blog in high rotation, re-issue of the cartoon series on DVD, or even being mentioned in a movie/TV show can up desirability of any line in a matter of hours. Figures and vehicles that wouldn't

COMMON TOY GRADES

One of the most contested aspects of the toy market is grading. Unlike coins and comic books, the lack of an impartial, third-party grader for toys leaves plenty of room for subjectivity that can either boost or lower a toy's value on the open market. Most of the toys that appear in this book have been offered at auction, and the prices are fair market values based on those sales. By default, these toys are usually graded "excellent" or "near mint" simply because it would be, on average, unprofitable for an auction house to try and sell anything in lesser grades. Nevertheless, collectors may use the following grading terms to rate collectible toys. Toys outside their original packaging are often referred to as "loose," especially action figures.

MINT IN BOX (MIB); MINT IN PACKAGE (MIP): Factory new, often still sealed as found on retail shelves. Boxes may have been opened, but any product or instructions remain unopened. Original boxes, blister packs, or tags, should remain intact and undamaged.

MINT NO PACKAGE (MNP); MINT NO BOX (MNB): Original package may be missing, but toy is complete and appears never to have been used; still retains all accessories in unused condition and tags are also complete and undamaged.

sell for .99 cents and free shipping start closing out at five times over what they originally cost at retail. Even blogs ... have had an effect on the desirability of a figure line."[5]

Provenance explains an established history of ownership. Once a vintage toy has entered the secondary market, it develops a provenance. A famous owner can add at most 15 percent or more on the value of a toy but there are exceptions and this changes dramatically depending on who owned the toy in the past. When Leonardo DiCaprio sold part of his action figure collection at Morphy Auctions in 2006, values were stronger than expected thanks to his famous name. It helped that the collection was "in killer condition," according to auctioneer

5 Khayos shares his opinions on action figure grading on ragingnerdgasm.com.

NEAR MINT (NM): Complete toy retaining original accessories but showing slight signs of use or shelf wear. Original box may be missing.

EXCELLENT (EXL): Toy is complete and shows signs of minor wear, very clean. Some paint flaking and minor chipping or crazing is acceptable, slight staining, original packaging missing. Don't be surprised to see this term applied to toys that survive 100 years or more – the older and more rare the toy, the more graders forgive imperfections or restoration.

VERY GOOD (VG): Obvious wear from a toy that has been played with: chipping paint, rust missing parts or accessories, original packaging missing.

GOOD (G/GD): Lots of evidence of play, dinged-up or dented, scratches, missing paint, replaced or missing parts or components, marks or mar to crucial surface paint (eyes, logos, symbols, etc), dirt and stains.

PLAY-WORN: This term is one often applied to metal toys, but I think it should be used more often for roughed-up toys found at flea markets and country auctions. This is a "well-loved" toy and might survive as a shell of its former self. Perhaps it's been repainted, is missing parts, etc. Values based on coincidence.

Prototype toys are highly collectible among toy buffs as they represent the genesis of popular toys. Many toy lines were scuttled once prototypes were inspected for quality and design. The prototypes shown here were made by the famous Marx toy company by dealer George Diller of Erie, Pa. *Courtesy of Jack Kelly*

Dan Morphy. The auction raised $110,000 for the actor's charity and saw a rare 1978 vinyl-caped Jawa *Star Wars* action figure end at $4,500.[6]

Quality may be a subjective criterion; however, a well-constructed toy is hard to find and fewer still survive for decades or even centuries. The more time you spend looking at quality toys, the easier it is to recognize good craftsmanship when you see it.

Condition is of the utmost importance in today's collector market. The most valuable items are in original condition with minimal restoration or alterations. This 'Best or Nothing' approach to condition has probably been the most influential change in the hobby during the last decade. Values of toys in mid-range to low condition have fallen, while values of rare toys in top condition often skyrocket beyond all expectations.

THE DIGITAL GENERATION

The popular nature of vintage toys and the veritable explosion of collector toys manufactured and marketed strictly to adults have resulted in an explosion of discussion about toys

---

6 The vinyl cape Jawa is one of the most expensive *Star Wars* figures of the vintage line and was produced in small quantities before it was replaced by Jawa with a cloth cape. It can still fetch a handsome sum outside its packaging.

This rare Walking Mechanical Pinocchio toy dates to the 1930s and can be found for less than **$250** with its rare original box. It stands 11" h, has a clockwork mechanism, and was made of composition material for the Geo. Borgfeldt Corp. of New York by the Lewis & Scott Mfg. Co., Inc. of Plantsville, Connecticut. Borgfeldt was not a manufacturer or a toy company, but was actually a distributor of toys and novelties to American stores. *Courtesy of Jack Kelly*

online. Google shows more than 300,000 toy-related blogs exist on the internet. Many of these blogs are connected to collectors' websites. These blogs share opinions, reviews, and release dates, and artist interviews on everything from action figures to American Girl Dolls.

The online community for toys doesn't end with blogs. For instance, the hot toy of Christmas 2013 was the Rainbow Loom, an interlocking rubber band system used to make bracelets and all sort of craft-type items. As of October 2014, YouTube.com displayed more than 2.9 million Rainbow Loom instruction videos. This level of interactive content boosted demand, which boosted sales, which in turn boosted the number of counterfeit products online and in some stores.

Collectors are constantly seeking sites such as blogs and YouTube to learn more about their favorite toys. This demand has also sparked a boon in specialized marketplaces that connect buyers with collectors. For many years, eBay.com was the go-to source for LEGO collectors to locate rare sets and minifigures, the yellow-tinted characters used in construction sets. At any one time, more than 350,000 lots of LEGO toys and collectibles are listed on eBay. But LEGO collectors have also migrated to BrickPicker.com, a top resource for investing and

Longtime collectors say the original box the toy came in almost always increases the value of the toy by a minimum of 25 percent. This Dick Tracy Copmobile regularly brings **$125** to **$150** at auction, but examples with the original box sell for as much as **$240**.
Courtesy of Jack Kelly

collecting, and BrickLink.com, which bills itself as the "unofficial LEGO marketplace" and boasts more than 315,000 unique members.

BrickLink (which charges a fee to sell through the site) offers more than 8.6 million lots available for sale as of September 2014. That beats eBay's offering by a whopping 24 to one. With its trove of sales data, BrickLink has even created a customizable price guide that compares and contrasts the last six month's worth of sales to lots available for sale on the site. Other price tracking sites are Brickset.com and BrickPicker.com, both of which compare and contrast values for sets old and new.

The increase for this new generation of toys is driven primarily by a generational shift and changing demand. As Millenials and Generation X begin to spend more on the toys of their youth, the values for items favored by Baby Boomers are decreasing in value.

Western Hero toys that were popular in the 1980s are seeing a marked decrease: The value of a Hopalong Cassidy shooting gallery in its original box has remained virtually unchanged for 30 years.[7] Perhaps it's because the collecting public hasn't seen

---

7 *The Official 1984 Price Guide to Collectible Toys*, pg. 552, states the value of this set as $60-$70, which, according to the U.S. Inflation Calculator, shows is worth roughly $137-$160 in 2014 dollars; four of six sets offered via LiveAuctioneers.com sold between $100 to $150 from 2010 and 2014, according to historical auction data.

a new Hopalong Cassidy product since 1950, when more than 100 companies produced an estimated $70 million worth of branded products.

On the flipside, some LEGO sets show after market values growing by 10 to 12 percent annually depending on the popularity of the set and its initial production run.[8] And Walt Disney's "Princess line" — composed of the leading ladies from several of Disney's animated features — now

Collectors seek odd and unusual toys, such as these car dealer toy promotional cars offered by dealer Bob Cline of Woodstock, Ill. Car dealerships and even service stations offered the cars to children in an attempt to get mom and dad on the showroom floor.
Courtesy of Jack Kelly

makes about $4 billion a year, on par with the earning power of Mickey Mouse himself.[9] Take a guess how the next generation of toy collectors will be "Letting Go" of their disposable income during the next 20 years.

Toy expert Mark Bellomo puts this (as well as the greater economic climate) in context in his book, *Toys & Prices*, when he says: "Toys that aren't in demand languish in retail aisles and gather dust on the pegs of secondary store walls, while it appears that many higher-end collectibles ... meet considerable resistance from buyers; these items just aren't getting the bids they used to receive." Bellomo advises profit-seeking toy collectors to think critically about resale potential based on the difference between "nostalgia value" and "retail value."[10]

When it comes to timing the market in order to sell, pickers owe it to their future profits to stake a claim at the corner of popular culture and near mint condition.

8 Market trend data shared by Anthony Bearden, Minifigs Bricks & More, Denton, TX
9 Appelbaum, Binyamin, "How Disney Turned 'Frozen' into its hottest cash cow," *New York Times*, Nov. 21, 2014.
10 *Toys & Prices: The World's Best Toys Price Guide*, 19th edition.

MICKEY THE MUSICAL MOUSE

This rare Mickey Mouse tin litho toy was the most valuable toy lot in Hake's Americana & Collectibles March 2014 auction, but it did not deliver the seller a return in his investment. Why? It perfectly illustrates how Authenticity, Exposure, Provenance, Quality, Condition all influence toy values and how changing demand are affecting the market. Here's how:

AUTHENTICITY

Produced in Germany for import to England, as noted by marking on underside, the toy is the best, rarest and most sought after of all German-made Mickey Mouse tin toys. The text on underside reads, "By Exclusive Arrangement With The Ideal Films Ltd." 1930. The main body of toy measures 3-1/8" h x 9-3/4" l.

EXPOSURE

Hake's catalogers proclaimed, "This is the only example of this toy we know of," placing this toy in the category of "Scarce." Non collectors may think this fact hurts a collectible's value, but to serious collectors, the scarcer a toy is, the more it is seen as a "Great White Buffalo" to the hobby.

PROVENANCE

The toy was purchased for $40,000 by Maurice Sendak, author of the classic, *Where the Wild Things Are*. At that price, Sendak likely purchased the toy at the height of the market demand for Mickey Mouse collectibles, the 1980s-1990s. It was auctioned directly from Sendak's collection and was accompanied by a Certificate of Authenticity.

QUALITY

Three different versions of this toy were produced; this version with Minnie Mouse is considered the best. For a Depression-era toy, the mechanism is quite sophisticated: Attached to the back of toy is a metal hand-crank box that when handle is turned, moves a painted tin arm which has three separate die-cut tin litho heads attached. When cranked, toy produces musical notes and heads move back and forth.

CONDITION

Scattered spider-webbing to tin litho surface of main toy body, not offensive. Heads have some scattered aging and spider-webbing to surfaces, with middle head being more moderately aged. Fine overall.

SALES PRICE?

$13,890 — a strong price, but below the house's $20,000 to $40,000 estimate.

So why did a great toy with all these winning attributes not deliver the same dollar value (or better yet, a return) on the original $40,000 purchase price? The answer, I think, is three fold.

First, the toy was purchased at the height of the demand for Mickey Mouse items.

Second, the toy is not a historically important contribution to the character or toy history in general.

Last but not least, the market for Mickey Mouse toy items is soft due to a changing taste among collectors. Mickey Mouse debuted in 1928 — fully 87 years ago — and the generation that once felt affinity for the character is not spending what they once did to own classic toys. Mickey Mouse also doesn't get the exposure his fellow Disney Universe characters have enjoyed the last ten to 15 years. Mickey Mouse — like Superman, Popeye, and other characters from the first half of the 20th century — will still remain popular with collectors ($13,980 is still a lot of money!), but all things must change and as younger collectors grow up, they turn their attention to familiar characters they themselves enjoyed as a child.

When determining a toy's value, it's helpful to think of values in ranges, rather than a fixed number, and to buy in the best condition you can afford. The secondary market is influenced by shifting demand, condition, and many other intangible factors. One of the most well-known American tin wind-up toys is Li'l Abner's Dogpatch Band. Made by Unique Art Manufacturing Co. in 1945, the toy is often found in excellent condition. This comical toy measures 8" h x 9" w and features all four of the main characters from the comic strip series. You can expect to pay between **$500** and **$600** for one in excellent to near mint condition; however, it pays to do some research before you start shopping. The toy (*below*) was found priced at **$600** at a Brimfield Antiques Show in Massachusetts. The toy (*above*) was sold with its original box at auction for **$537**. The "show special" is in much worse condition than the one sold at auction, although it is priced 10 percent more. Which one do you think has a better chance at holding its value over the long term? An educated shopper would know they have plenty of "haggle room" at a show, but it would be a better investment to save the money and buy an example in top condition in the first place.

Photo above courtesy of Heritage Auctions; photo below courtesy of Eric Bradley

Original boxes make a huge difference to collectible toy values. This pre-World War II windup toy was made in Japan of celluloid and is marked "Donald Duck Walt Disney Japan" on back and still retains the original inspection sticker on Donald's stomach. Mickey, Minnie, Donald, and Pluto characters on umbrella (above Donald's head), includes coveted original box as distributed by George Borgfeldt. It sold for **$950** at auction. The same toy without the original box brings **$750** at auction. *Courtesy of Morphy Auctions*

This one of a kind German Kris Kringle doll is covered by approximately 55 period playthings, offering an extraordinary glimpse of Christmas in 1852. When it was offered from the collection of noted doll expert Richard Wright in 2010, bidders ignored its $6,000 pre-auction estimate and pushed the sale price to **$14,220**.

Courtesy of Skinner Auctions, Inc., www.skinnerinc.com

Toys that exist to defy imagination (or are just plain absurd) are the most sought after – such as this 12" long, 1950s-era toy featuring Superman riding a motorcycle. This odd Spaceman Superman Cycle is a Japanese friction toy retaining its ultra rare original box. The box is marked "Bandai, Made in Japan" and "617." The cycle is tin litho and has a scarce figure of Superman made of hard rubber and vinyl cape. This example still has the almost impossible to find tin litho Superman shield on chest, mainly because this toy is considered "old store stock," as it was discovered in a toy store in Japan. It's possibly the best known example and it sold for **$55,200** at auction. *Courtesy of Morphy Auctions*

Tin toy, circa 1910, made by Marklin, Dredger with Fountain, No. 4235, embossed tin, hand-painted, crank drive, 20" h, **$4,300**. *Courtesy of Auction Team Breker*

CHAPTER 3

Tin Toys

In 1887, a Brooklyn man identified only as Mr. Thomass, owner of Thomass' Tin Toy Co., gave a detailed explanation on how his seven-person, three-story factory produced a single tin toy horse:

"The first thing in my business is to make the design of the toy to be manufactured. The outlines are cut in card board, and from this the stencil is made in metal which is laid on the tin, and by one slip of a press is cut into shape. Each toy you see here must pass through many hands before it is perfected. Two shapes must be cut from the metal. Then the contours must be rounded out by another workman, and the two parts are soldered together exactly. A platform with little wheels must be made to place the horse on, but first the horse must be painted. Several large vats of different colored paints are ready to dip the toys in when necessary. It takes but a moment for the workman to immerse the horse in the liquid, when … it is carried to a drying room. Later it is given to a facial artist for the coloring of the eyes, nostrils, mane and tail; still another workman fastens the horse to the platform and bell on its back, or perchance a jockey"[11]

Tellingly, the article does not identify Mr. Thomass as a "toy maker" but rather as an artist. Collectors would easily agree that his creations, and those of his generation, were the first to bridge the gap between toys and art.

Precious little information survives from the dawn of America's tin toy factories. Francis, Field and Francis (aka the Philadelphia Tin Toy Manufactory) opened a tin plate kitchenware factory on South Market Street in Philadelphia in 1838. By the early 1840s it had expanded into toys such as tin and iron wagons and floor trains. Unfortunately, the makers of many early American tin toys are unknown and the very early toys are often unattributed. Collectors are not discouraged by this lack

---

11 *Wichita Eagle*, July 9, 1887, Page 6, reprinted from the *Brooklyn Eagle*.

of information. On the contrary, the fraternal community of tin toy collectors is generous with its research.

Tin toys "never really fell out of popularity," says Michael Bertoia, auctioneer at Bertoia Auctions, the New Jersey auction house that has sold tens of thousands of tin toys over the last 40 years. "Between transportation toys such as cars, planes, and trains to whimsical, Disney-type toys from the USA to Japan, or clockwork/wind-up animated tin toys from France or Germany, tin toys have always been a popular item. There are collectors in all corners of the world."

The tin toy market has seen three important changes revolutionize values: condition, the onset of internet bidding, and the recent release of major collections.

INTERNET MEANS ACCESS

The onset of internet and online bidding changed the hobby immeasurably. At the height of the 2014 holiday shopping season, more than 45,000 tin toys were offered for sale on the online marketplace eBay. Specialty auctions, dominated by east coast auctioneers, offered another 3,000 high-end examples in online-assisted live auctions in the fall of 2014. This seemingly crushing amount of inventory did nothing to affect both prices and sell-through rates, which remained high. "When you consider the number of tin toys sold at auction today it seems like a large number." Bertoia said. "But one has to keep in mind that

America's first factory-produced toy: Philadelphia's Francis, Field and Francis is credited as the first commercial toy maker in the United States. This colossal, 22-inch long tin Conestoga wagon toy is a rare survivor from Antebellum America. It sold at a June 2014 auction for **$6,325.** *Courtesy of RSL Auction Company*

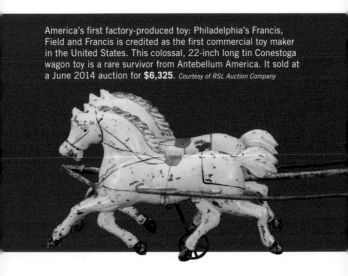

With the perspective gained from the last 170 years, early American tin toy "factories" were more akin to workshops, the likes of which today we only see in artists' collectives and ultra small-scale boutiques. These three toys were all produced (by hand) in these workshops and, although unattributed, they resemble the type of toy that would have been produced in the Brooklyn workshop of Thomass' Tin Toys.

Tin Toy, circa 1880, maker unknown, American, one toy 4" l, other with jockey 6-1/2" l, **$183**.
Courtesy of RSL Auction Company

Tin toy, circa 1880, maker unknown, American, 6-1/6" l, **$376**.
Courtesy of RSL Auction Company

Tin toy, circa 1885, possibly Merriam Toy Co., Connecticut, 4-1/2" l, **$796**.
Courtesy of RSL Auction Company

in the 1970s, 1980s, and 1990s, antique toy shows and fairs were very prevalent and well attended throughout the world and the number of tin toys sales at such shows was probably very large as well. With that said, a regionally focused toy show had much less accessibility and awareness when compared to an antique toy auction in today's marketplace."

FLOODING NOT A WORRY

Longtime tin toy collectors are not worried about large scale, important collections "flooding the market" and depressing prices in the short term. In the case of tin toys, when high-grade examples are released back to collectors, values are only on the upswing.

Among these important collections to have come to market in the last decade include K·B Toys founder Donald Kaufman's automotive toy collection; the collection of Washington D.C. lawyer Max Berry holding one of the world's finest assemblages of bell toys, cast iron drawn horses, and early tin toys, plus European penny toys; and the antique boats and nautical toy collection of chemical wholesaler and author Richard T. Claus brought several high-grade examples to market within six years of each other. Collections like these do not come up very often. The opportunity was unprecedented. "I can confidently say that there have been some tin toys offered out in the past decade which haven't been seen by the public since the middle of the 20th century!" said Bertoia. "Talk about the right place at the right time."

Lifelong collector and tin toy expert David Pressland, author of the landmark, *The Art of the Tin Toy* (Crown, 1976), agrees that the amount of toys on the market just means collectors have more to love. "There is a lot on the market at the moment and this has given opportunities for new collectors to both inspect and buy pieces that they might never have seen in the flesh," Pressland said.

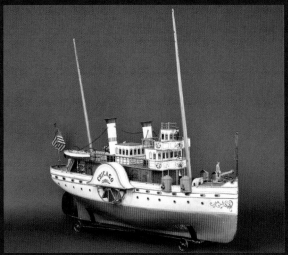

Tin toy, circa 1900-1902, Germany, made by Marklin, "Providence Paddle Wheel" ship, #1071, artistic appointments at cabin windows with painted curtains and ornately stamped seating area: second level with passenger benches and bridge have gold painted railing, funnel is held steady by chains to deck, lifeboats hang on davits, boarding area ready with opening plank door, covered paddle wheels proudly read "PROVIDENCE," with accent lines, a first class clockwork powered example of a significant toy importance, from the collection of Dick Claus, 26" l, **$247,250**. *Courtesy of Bertoia Auctions*

Tin toy, circa 1900-1902, Germany, by Marklin, "Chicago" Paddle Wheel ship, #1080/2, tiered decks and platforms are enveloped by fine railing appointments, and all levels contain composition full figures, featured on the dust cover of the book, *Allure of Toy Ships*, hand-painted lower deck curtains, blue and brown band stacks and matching paddle wheel covers, side guns all hanging lifeboats at the ready, with six original figures of the Captain and crew, toy exudes luxury with the utmost artistic perfection: the complex bridge structure, enormous bow and coupled with original tall wood mast put this clockwork example in a class by itself, from the collection of Dick Claus, 31" l, **$264,500**. *Courtesy of Bertoia Auctions*

KEYS TO TIN TOY COLLECTING

1. Take opportunities as and when they arise. There are still constant surprises, especially with 19th century toys and if an item has quality, appeals and is in the right condition it should be bought even if it is not on your 'shopping list.'
2. Always buy the best quality and condition that you can afford.
3. Learn from your mistakes.
4. Be very careful in attempting to clean or restore a toy yourself. It is always best to leave it in its virgin, as found state than try to over clean and lose patina. Simple cleaning with enzymatic fluid (commonly known as spit) soaked cotton buds will do no harm and works well. This can be followed by a light polish.

Used with permission from Art of the Tin Toy, artofthetintoy.com

"It has also tended to polarize the market with the very rare and desirable pieces in good, original condition making very strong prices and ordinary pieces in mediocre condition making seemingly low prices - although common pieces in pristine condition are still doing well."

CONDITION IS KING

"The biggest factor impacting the current collecting climate is condition," Bertoia said. "The best condition pieces continue to increase in value through time."

Influenced by both the auctions of important collections as well as lightning-fast communication thanks to the internet, collectors have keenly zeroed in on condition as the market's supreme qualifier. As soon as the first tin toys were offered on eBay, collectors realized that age doesn't always mean value and rarity was often defined by your circle of confidants. Examples graded in excellent condition or better quickly find a new home.

This doesn't mean most tin toys are five figure gems – three times as many tin toys sell between $100 and $500 than they do priced between $500 and $5,000.[12]

"Today's collectors have the fantastic opportunity of buying

---

12 LiveAuctioneers prices realized data, 1999, 2003-2014.

a quality piece which may have taken the prior owner 30 years of scouring the globe to encounter, Bertoia said. "A collector can now buy a tin toy without having to travel far lengths, they can have the reassurance that the item is as described, and for most people they can feel comfortable that they are paying a fair market price in a public forum."

WHERE TO FIND THEM

Given these factors influencing values, today's tin toy buyers and sellers face two bedrock rules before you start your hunt:

1. You must be brutally honest with yourself about condition.

If your fellow collectors and dealers use price guides and free internet searches to compare and contrast values, there is no future in presenting a toy in *good* condition as an *excellent* or *near mint* no matter how old it may be.

2. Buy and sell ordinary and lesser-quality pieces at values based on you and your customers' cost to find a similar example.

You have to understand which toys are rare and which toys are ordinary. The history of the tin toy spans at least 180 years. Steam-operated toys are much rarer than wind-up examples. It's incumbent to assemble a library of important reference books (how-to guides, reference books, auction catalogs, museum exhibition programs) in order to educate yourself on what is truly "rare." Every piece can then be put into some type of census context based on the number of pieces known to exist.

Tin toy, circa 1912, Germany, made by Marklin. Considered the finest in Marklin's range of toys, this Steam Fire Truck is a stunning masterpiece in overall detail, from bright hand-painted open frame with exposed boiler, to its many added appointments, powered by live steam, it produces pressure to release water from valves, the intricate gear work in open frame is a marvel of ingenuity, scarce: less than five are known of to date, figures added to truck, from the Don Kaufman Collection, 18" l, **$149,500**. *Courtesy of Bertoia Auctions*

Tin toy, circa 1910s, maker unknown, bar with composition barman (bartender), hand-painted room set with shaped bar and tinplate drinks dispensers, shelves to back and side walls, large bar sign above and composition bartender, excellent, 13-3/4" h, **$650-$700**. *Courtesy of Bonhams*

Tin toy, circa late 1800s, Flapping Wing Airplane, Germany, Made by Fisher, oversized tin litho, original driver, all original celluloid propellers (when in operation, propellers turn and front wings flap up and down), unique and unusual, excellent, 20" l, **$6,600**. *Courtesy of Morphy Auctions*

Tin Play Grocery set, with nice 1930s-era painted graphics, and an incredible assortment of miniature product boxes, all in Very Good condition, dimensions unknown, **$50-$125**. *Courtesy of Heritage Auctions*

Tin toy, circa 1910, Bing, coastal gun, cast iron base and canon with tin armor, hand-painted, for rubber shells, can turn and tilt in any direction, 10-1/4" l, **$3,400**. *Courtesy of Auction Team Breker*

Tin toy, racing game, by Jeannette Toy & Novelty Co. tin litho, "Brownie Auto Race," marble roll game set, featuring early auto racing image, complete metal auto playing pieces, excellent, 10-1/2" dia, **$287**. *Courtesy of William Morford Investment Grade Collectibles at Auction*

Meier Triumph penny toy, Germany, pre-1914, motorbike with sidecar, very good, **$9,349**.

Courtesy of Antico Mondo, LiveAuctioneers

PENNY TOYS

Penny Toys are just that: small tinplate toys once sold in stores for a penny. They were most prolific in America and Europe, especially Germany, between 1895 and 1914. The deceptively simple toys rank among the most popular tinplate toys and are widely collected all over the world.

Popularly collected manufacturers include Johann Distler of Germany, Carette of France, and J. Ph. Meier in Nuremberg. The diversity is astounding: ranging from occupational figures, ships, carriages and locomotives, the toys usually offered some moving parts or even noisemaking capabilities. Like any toy, the more elaborate or exotic the theme the more collectors will compete to own it.

In 1987, Christie's specifically listed penny toys as among its hot sellers in its London saleroom, especially those made in Nuremberg at the turn of the century. Interest has only grown since then. Thousands have been sold at auction since 2003 with most selling between $100 and $500, according to LiveAuctioneers.com. The most valuable penny toys sold since 2008 include a circa 1914 German Meier Triumph motorbike with sidecar with three riders sold for $9,349; a German Meier Father Christmas figure pulling a sleigh sold for $5,000; and a clockwork German HMN "Autos and Airplanes" Roundabout toy, with four open tourer penny toys with seated drivers, and four silver painted monocoupes, also sold for $5,000.

Airship Penny Toy, French, early 1900s, all painted and japanned tin, incised at end of whistle tube "Made In France," desirable early airship design with suspended basket, whistle tube and air hole in middle of tube creates sound and revolves japanned tin propellers, scarce, 4" l x 2" h, **$345**.
Courtesy of Hakes Americana & Collectibles

Diridible Penny Toy, Germany, circa 1920s, unmarked but believed by Distler, tin litho retaining nice details including crew members in the two gondolas, original string mechanism with pair of metal finger loops (when the bottom loop is pulled, it causes the dirigible to ascend up the string as the large propeller rotates), scarce, 1" x 1-1/2" x 6" l, **$632**. *Courtesy of Hakes Americana & Collectibles*

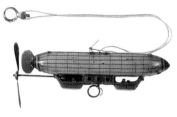

Train Penny Toy with original box, painted tin with cast metal wheels, unmarked, 1880s-1890s, original box has recipient's name written in script on lid, fine, 3" l, **$347**. *Courtesy of Hakes Americana & Collectibles*

Billiard Player Penny Toy, Germany, circa 1920s, tin litho by Kellermann, pool player has spring-loaded cue stick and top surface of table has recessed scoring areas (these penny toys were originally issued with metal cover at one corner to hold the steel ballbearing in place but was then intended to be removed to use the toy and this example is complete with cover intact), 1-1/2" x 4" x 2-3/8" h, **$230**. *Courtesy of Hakes Americana & Collectibles*

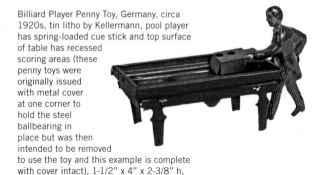

Fire Pumper Penny Toy, Germany, pre-1914, marked Distler, tin litho, this is the longer of two version of this pumper that was made, fine, 4-1/4" l, **$258**. *Courtesy of Hakes Americana & Collectibles*

Horse-drawn Cart Penny Toy, Germany, circa 1910s, marked "ges. gesch" (to signify the toy or part of it is covered under German patent), excellent, scarce, 4-1/2" l, **$230**.
Courtesy of Hakes Americana & Collectibles

Tractor Penny Toy, Germany, pre-1914, made by Distler, long tin litho marked "Made In Germany," detailed lithography on both sides of engine, fine, 3-3/4" l, **$230**. *Courtesy of Hakes Americana & Collectibles*

Wind-up toy, made by Steiff, Teddy Roosevelt on horseback, Teddy with a composition painted head and dressed in his Rough Rider military outfit with original gloves, boots, and hat, sits atop his Appaloosa, with a Steiff button in his ear, rare, 38" l x 27" h, **$7,170**.

Courtesy of Heritage Auctions

ALWAYS A CUSTOMER: WIND-UP TIN TOYS

Wind-up toys are one of the largest segments of the tin toy hobby. They are presented here to help you see the difference between early American and European examples and the much more widely available, 20th century American and Japanese cousins.

You might hear these toys referred to by two different names: *clockwork* and/or *wind-up*. These toys are powered by a mainspring-driven motor and tinplate gears, and are ostensibly considered wind-ups or clockworks. The phrase *clockwork* is the used adjective to refer to these wind-up toys, although

Wind-up toy set, circa 1950s, Schuco, includes a monkey violinist, monkey drummer, and a pair of monkeys lifting a mouse, excellent, 4-1/2" h, **$425.25**.

Courtesy of James D. Julia Auctioneers, Fairfield, Maine, www.jamesdjulia.com

many do not feature true, highly sophisticated clock mechanisms as the phrase would suggest. They all receive their energy through accessory keys or fixed cranks used to manually wind the mainspring.

The first American wind-up toys were made by George W. Brown and Co. in 1856. The next 50 years saw European firms, such as Bing, Arnold, and Tippco Toys specialize and collectors now gravitate to their steam ships, ocean liners, zeppelins and novelty figures. France's Carette Company used clockwork mechanisms for their intricately-detailed vehicle toys, ranging from limousines to Mercedes open touring cars and collectors often pay between $3,000 and $6,000 for examples in excellent condition. The importance of the wind-up mechanism can't be understated and it was the dominate form of locomotion until the battery-powered revolution of the late 1950s.

This diversity, themes, and mechanism variations of tin toys is immense – during the peak holiday shopping season last year, eBay sellers offered more than 20,000 tin wind-up toys. The principles ruling collector values of all toys (condition, rarity, authenticity, exposure) also apply to wind-ups; however, the extreme diversity means there's a collector for every imaginable combination. Values tend to remain steady and show no signs of faltering. The top of the market is dominated by high-grade examples from a variety of subjects: a rare Tippco Mickey Mouse and Minnie Mouse motorcycle, circa 1932, (a rare example from one of the earliest German toy makers) sold for $67,000 in 2010.

Commando Joe Mechanical Crawling Soldier (Ohio Art, c. 1940s). An 8" Ohio Art tin lithograph, wind-up Commando Joe Mechanical Crawling Soldier with its original box. The toy is in Excellent condition, with only a few small scrapes and the box is in Fine condition with normal storage wear for a toy of this age. From the Don Vernon Collection, **$40**. *Courtesy of Heritage Auctions*

Wind-up, G. I. Joe and His Jouncing Jeep Mechanical Tin Toy by Unique Art Mfg. Co., Inc., toy bounces Joe off of his seat as the vehicle putters along, fine, many variants exist, 3" w x 7" l x 8" h, **$100-$200**, with original box brings **$550-$600** at auction. *Courtesy of Heritage Auctions*

WIND-UP VS FRICTION

What's the Difference Between Wind-up Toys and Friction Toys?

FRICTION TOYS use a form of pullback motor, which winds up an internal coil spring. The toy is pulled back and when released, it is propelled forward by the spring. Once the spring is unwound, the motor is disengaged by a clutch and the toy can then roll forward freely. D.P. Clark, a member of a Dayton, Ohio, group of toymakers, is credited for inventing the process in 1897. Another form of friction toys uses a large flywheel connected to drive wheels via a low gear ration. These types of toys can be "revved up" by pushing the car repeatedly forward.

WIND-UP TOYS first appeared in the 15th century. Even Leonardo da Vinci created a wind-up toy lion. Watch-like in their construction, the toys feature a central spring wound through the manual turning of a key extending from the toy. As the energy in the spring is released, it moves a series of interconnecting gears, causing any manner of activity. By the 1950s, wind-up toys were replaced by battery-operated toys. More expensive clockwork toys first appeared around 1860, but they fell out of favor by the turn of the century due to advancements in inexpensive tinplate gears.

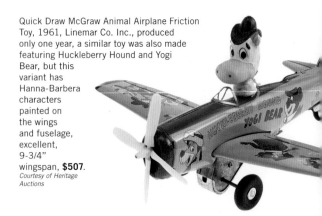

Quick Draw McGraw Animal Airplane Friction Toy, 1961, Linemar Co. Inc., produced only one year, a similar toy was also made featuring Huckleberry Hound and Yogi Bear, but this variant has Hanna-Barbera characters painted on the wings and fuselage, excellent, 9-3/4" wingspan, **$507**.
Courtesy of Heritage Auctions

Hopping Quick Draw McGraw Tin Toy, 1962, Louis Marx & Co. Inc., mechanical wind-up, hopping, tin toy, uncommon, excellent, **$100-$200**.
Courtesy of Heritage Auctions

Wyandotte Toys Humphrey Mobile Wind-up Toy, tin litho, Wyandotte maker's mark on top, 8-1/4" l x 7-1/4" h, **$200-$300**.

Courtesy of Heritage Auctions

Wind-up, tin litho, maker unknown but possibly H. Fischer & Co., marked "Made in Germany" with American and British patents and German D.R.P.A. marks on bottom of toy, 7" h, **$700-$800**.
Courtesy of Heritage Auctions

Wind up toy, Made in Germany, circa 1900s, maker unknown, tin litho figure, built-in key on side and wheels next to feet pushing 4" dia, double hoop, 6" h, **$747**. *Courtesy of Bertoia Auctions*

Wind-up toy, 1925, made by Ferdinand Strauss Corp. New York, No. 41, tin litho, depicts Boob standing full figure with note on his back, "I'm Boob McNutt R. L. Goldberg," accompanied by thin cardboard box and signed at lower right by cartoonist R.L. Goldberg. Side panels each feature a different daily comic strip with Boob, box: 2-3/4" x 4" x 9" h; toy: 8-3/4" h, **$670.45**. *Courtesy of Bertoia Auctions*

Wind-up, 1920s-1930s, Marx, tin litho, four mice with cone-shaped faces each are either dancing or playing a musical instrument, sitting/ standing about an upright piano. Even the piano is lithographed with various mice on all three sides, box pictures many different mice in a stage setting, working, a classic American tin toy considered a staple for every collection, 9-1/2" w x 9" h, **$1,125.75**.

Courtesy of James D. Julia Auctioneers, Fairfield, Maine, www.jamesdjulia.com

Wind-up, made by Lehman, Man Da Rin, a classic German tin toy, two coolies clockwork motor hidden in sedan chair as mandarin tugs the leading coolie's pigtail, includes very scarce original box with very little wear. Toy depicts Chinese men carrying another man in cart, original hairpieces, classic German tin toy, excellent, 7-1/4" l, **$14,500**. *Courtesy of Morphy Auctions*

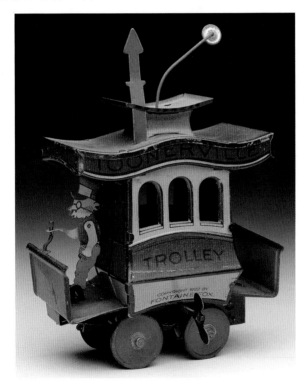

Wind-up, 1922, made by Nifty (H. Fischer & Co.) Nuremberg, Germany, train car from Fontaine Fox's American comic strip rolls along with moving driver at tiller, complete and original with smokestack and driver, excellent, 7" h, **$355** (sets with original tracks and boxes bring **$4,000+** at auction).

Courtesy of James D. Julia Auctioneers, Fairfield, Maine, www.jamesdjulia.com

Doll, France, circa 1916, character doll by Albert Marque, #27 of only 100 models known to have been made, bisque socket head, highly artistic sculpting with a unique four-part mold used only for this doll, amber brown glass paperweight eyes, brunette mohair wig, original uniquely modeled body, marks: A. Marque (incised signature) 27 (inscribed number on head) (partial pencil label on foot, see photo) Margaine-Lacroix 19 Boulevard Haussman Paris (cloth label in costume), original couturier-sewn costume (doll was considered the keynote piece of the Stein am Rhein Museum), excellent, 22" h, **$300,000**. *Courtesy of Theriault's Antique Doll Auctions*

CHAPTER 4

Dolls and Teddy Bears

Few collectible toy categories are as sensitive to condition and provenance than dolls and plush toys, including teddy bears. Both have seen a tremendous decrease in the number of new collectors to the hobby. Both were acutely affected by the 2008 global economic downturn, which spooked deep-pocketed buyers and convinced longtime collectors to hold on to their collections until the climate improved. Sentiment is improving – albeit slowly – but the market for mid-range and low-end dolls and plush toys still has not returned to the robust sales seen 15 years ago. In this category, it's important for buyers to make a decision early on: Collect for fun or save the cash and collect for returns.

HEAR STEIFF ROAR

Few dolls evoke such a strong emotion than the teddy bear. There's a reason why they are the go-to toy from hospital gift shops to high-end department stores. One of the hottest toys for the 2014 holiday season was a massive 93-inch, 48-1/2 pound, teddy bear named "Hugfun" sold through Costco. The price? $290 retail – but a whopping $760 on the collector's market once it was sold out.

Picker's Tip

Steiff teddy bears with rod jointing were only produced for a small number of years and very few remain today.

Teddy bears are a uniquely American creation; the toy was invented in honor of U.S. President Teddy Roosevelt. In 1902, political cartoonist Clifford Berryman immortalized a story in which Roosevelt refused to shoot a bound black bear following a disappointing day hunting. Brooklyn, New York, candy shop owners Morris Michtom and his wife, Rose, quickly revamped their small plush toy business and sought the President's permission to use his name on their line of "teddy bears." The toys were such a windfall for the couple that they soon founded the Ideal Toy Company, one of the world's largest doll producers.

Whereas Americans invested the teddy bear, perhaps it was the German company Steiff that perfected them. Begun by Margarete Steiff in 1880, the firm was in the stuffed elephant business before launching their teddy bear line in 1902. By 1907, the company was producing 974,000 bears for worldwide export. Fakes are found out by missing the firm's trademark "button in ear," started in 1904, which changed through the years but now allows collectors to date the toys that survive.

Teddy Bear, oldest Steiff teddy bear design known, blond mohair bear, rod jointed, the second type of jointing Steiff experimented with at the very early turn of the last century, 5-ways jointed, and has felt paw pads (he originally would have had five black claw stitches on each paw; he is missing a few stitches on his left hand paw), black shoebutton eyes, a shaved muzzle, a black hand-formed gutta percha nose, and a light brown mouth, original elephant button in his ear, perhaps the most desirable Steiff ID in the world, from the Chuck & Cathy Steffes Collection, 15" h, **$14,220**. *Courtesy of James D. Julia Auctioneers, Fairfield, Maine, www.jamesdjulia.com*

One of the Most Valuable Bears Ever Sold

One of the most sought after vintage Steiff bears in the world: Only 655 total of these red-backed-eye bears were produced in response to the sinking of the Titanic in 1912 and only 78 were made in this size and mohair configuration. This teddy bear is made from black mohair and is 5-ways jointed with tan felt paw pads and solidly stuffed with excelsior. Teddy's face is detailed with highly distinctive red felt backed shoe-button eyes and a black hand-embroidered nose and mouth, bear retains long trailing "F" button and a slight trace of his white tag. The red was to indicate crying and sadness at the extent of the tragedy, 12-1/2" h, **$35,550**. From the Chuck & Cathy Steffes Collection. *Courtesy of James D. Julia Auctioneers, Fairfield, Maine, www. jamesdjulia.com*

Among the devoted collectors of Steiff toys was Chuck and the late Cathy Steffes of Galax, Virginia, who focused their collection from the late 1800s through the early 1950s. When the collection was sent to James D. Julia Auctioneers in Fairfield, Maine, in June 2014, a selection of 120 bears, Mickey Mouse dolls, and rare cats hammered for nearly $500,000.

The cornerstone of the collection was a rod-jointed bear considered Steiff's oldest teddy bear design. Sales were strong across the board and were a market highlight of the last 15 years.

Despite the collection's strong emphasis on quality, most all of the teddy bears sold within expectations. It was a different story for the Steffes' collection of rare cats and rabbit. Those Steiff dolls soared past estimates, mainly due to rarity. "There are lots of bears, but certainly there are fewer cats and rabbits," said Andrew Truman, department head for Julia's Antique Advertising, Toy and Doll division.[13]

Even in the world of friendly teddy bears, the true competition for financial value exists among the scarce examples.

DOLL VALUES AT THE HIGH END

The year 2014 saw bidders set – and quickly shatter – a five-year world record for the most expensive doll sold at auction. In March 2014, the record was set when a boy doll crafted by sculptor Albert Marque of Paris sold for $300,000. The circa 1916 character doll, whose highly artistic sculpting is achieved by a unique four-part mold, is important because it exemplifies a deliberate and highly motivated movement that took place in early 20th century France to re-invigorate the French doll industry. The movement involved sculptors, porcelain firms, fashion designers and virtually the entire art community toward a common goal: to design a new type of doll, one that reflected the actual expressions and moods of childhood rather than the idealized "bebe dolls" of the late 19th century. The bebe doll was introduced by French doll maker Jumeau in 1877 and his style incorporates stylized chubby, rosy cheeks and large eyes. The dolls were made by the thousands for the international market at are avidly collected today.

The record-breaking Marque doll was sold by Theriault's, a doll specialty auction house founded in 1970 based in Annapolis,

13 Johnson, Elizabeth, "Julia sells titanic collection of Steiff," *Antique Week*, August 18, 2014.

Maryland. Theriault's made headlines in July 2009 when it sold an Albert Marque French antique doll to a Boston collector for $263,000.

"The A. Marque is the one name that carries the absolute allure for doll collectors all over the world. It is a work of art more than a doll," Theriault's President Stuart Holbrook told me. "It was a whole new concept at the time." Holbrook said he never questioned whether 2009 was the right year to bring the doll to auction, given the world's troubling economic climate. He knew the top of the market always commands top prices and credited the record to a changing attitude towards collecting: Quantity is out and quality is all that matters.

"The very high end will always see high prices," he said. "As any collector should be, one must be focused on their ability to get the best. A collection shouldn't be about numbers. It should be about quality: the absolute best."

Holbrook said recent prices show collectors are coming back into the market and the future is bright for exceptional examples. "While the very top pieces have been doing outstanding the past few years, the mid-range and more entry level pieces have been somewhat lagging behind and inconsistent," he said. "Over the past six-months we have seen these categories begin to come back in pricing ... for the first time since the financial crises of 2008. Collectors are coming back in droves and with a pent-up enthusiasm that is driving the market forward as we have never witnessed before."

Theriault's held the auction record for five years before breaking it in March 2014. It took just six months before the record would fall, this time by Bonhams, the London-headquartered auction house. An extraordinarily life-like little girl doll made by German doll manufactures Kämmer & Reinhardt, wearing a white dress and a blue ribbon sash, sold for $380,169. The doll's molded bisque head is attached to an eight ball jointed wood and composition body with swivel wrists and voice box.

The doll was not seen at auction for 20 years, after Sotheby's sold it in February of 1994 for $275,495 (roughly the equivalent of $426,500 in 2014 dollars).

If you take a critical look at these high-flying values, you'll begin to understand where the doll market has been the last 20 years. The Kämmer & Reinhardt, although a new world record, only increased in value by roughly $29,000 – or just 6 percent. Investment wise, that's a poor return but indicative on the generally low demand plaguing the market. Leigh Gotch, the head of Bonhams toy department, said collectors are likely to pay top dollar for especially rare dolls.

"We knew that the market has been a bit strange over the last few years but we also knew these were such very rare dolls … and they very rarely come together in one sale. The buyers are saying show us the best and they will still pay top prices – less people perhaps than before but the appetite is still there. You ask yourself if the marketplace can sustain this number of rare dolls, but at the end of the day it did."[14]

NOW IS THE TIME TO BUY

The doll market has seen a dramatic shift from antique to vintage during the last 15 years. Changing tastes and popular culture, along with demographic differences, now see vintage Barbie dolls produced in the 1950s sell for as much or more than rare bisque dolls from the 1800s. In the fall of 2014, a rare Bru Jeune No. 3 doll, with a leather body and composition legs, was sold by a collector in Japan via eBay for $16,101. Examples of the original Barbie doll, introduced in 1959 as both a blonde and a brunette, routinely bring $10,000-$15,000 at auction.

These sales are influenced by condition and provenance, of course, but pickers must be sure to focus on the rare and unusual if they want to see a return on their investments. Whereas a standard new Barbie doll costs roughly $5 retail, contemporary adult collector dolls can trade for thousands of dollars. "Barbie Lagerfeld," a limited edition doll dressed in Karl Lagerfeld's signature style, represents Mattel's attention to adult collectors. Available globally on September 29, 2014, the doll wears a tailored black jacket, white high-collared men's shirt with French cuffs and a black satin cravat finished off with fitted black jeans. Only 999 Platinum-label Barbie Lagerfeld

14 McKay, Ian, "Letter from London," *Maine Antique Digest*, December 2014, 20-D.

"Barbie Lagerfeld,"
a limited edition
doll dressed in Karl
Lagerfeld's signature
style, only 999
Platinum Label dolls
produced, **$1,000-
$1,400.**

dolls were produced and they retailed for approximately $200. By the end of the day of their release, the dolls were trading for as much as $2,000 each on eBay. A few months after the release, prices hover around $1,000 to $1,400.

Barbie might face some stiff competition in the coming years: The prices of American Girl Dolls have already surpassed four figures in online auctions. Targeted to girls ages eight to 12, the dolls debuted in 1986 by the Pleasant Company, which was bought by Mattel in 1998. Mint condition members of the original *Historical Characters* line of 18-inch dolls – Samantha, Kirsten and Molly – are now selling for four times their $100 original retail price in online auctions. The future is bright for

Remarkable and complete Brown Tipped Steiff Teddy Clown Bear, 5-ways jointed, excelsior stuffed and made from brown tipped mohair with peach-colored felt paw pads, original Steiff identification including his named, metal rimmed chest tag, larger long trailing "F" Steiff button and crisp and fully red, legible ear tag, working squeaker (this pattern was only in the line from 1926-1930 and was also produced in pink and yellow mohair), rare, Chuck & Cathy Steffes Collection, 12" h, **$26,662.50**.

Courtesy of James D. Julia Auctioneers, Fairfield, Maine, www.jamesdjulia.com

complete, mint-condition characters as the children who first collected these dolls begin hitting their late 30s and early 40s in 2015.

According to Sherry Minton, a longtime doll columnist with *Antique Trader Magazine*, the doll market suffered a massive hit following the 2008 global "Great Recession." Sales slowed and interest scaled back but appreciation for quality materials and history still brings collectors to auctions and shows. "There is plenty of supply on the market right now, allowing collectors to pick and choose. Perfect examples are still bringing top dollar while mediocre examples stay on the table," she said. "Now is the time to buy."

Teddy bear, Steiff, circa 1910, 5-ways jointed, firmly stuffed, and made from long curly gold mohair, exceptionally long arms, long narrow feet, and a pronounced back hump, working growler, bear sold with photo of his original owners and a letter explaining his history, bear has his small trailing "F" button and remnants of his white ear tag as his Steiff IDs, very good, from the Chuck & Cathy Steffes Collection, 24" h, **$21,330**.

Courtesy of James D. Julia Auctioneers, Fairfield, Maine, www.jamesdjulia.com

Extremely rare and very early velvet Steiff Rattle Cat With Elephant Button, circa 1905, unjointed, made from white velvet that has been painted with black and grey spots and stripes, early elephant style button attached to the red ribbon, Cat also has a rattle in its belly; Steiff created this feature by inserting a tube with beads into the torso of the item, design appeared overall in the Steiff line in 6, 8, 10, 12, and 14 cm in white and grey velvet from 1899 through 1929, from the Chuck & Cathy Steffes Collection, 4" h, **$7,702**. *Courtesy of James D. Julia Auctioneers, Fairfield, Maine, www.jamesdjulia.com*

Teddy bear, 1950s-era classic, 5-ways jointed blond bear with a stocky build, prominent and fuzzy muzzle, retains original blue ribbon and raised script button and worn yellow ear tag as his Steiff IDs, very good, 9" h, **$273**. *Courtesy of James D. Julia Auctioneers, Fairfield, Maine, www.jamesdjulia.com*

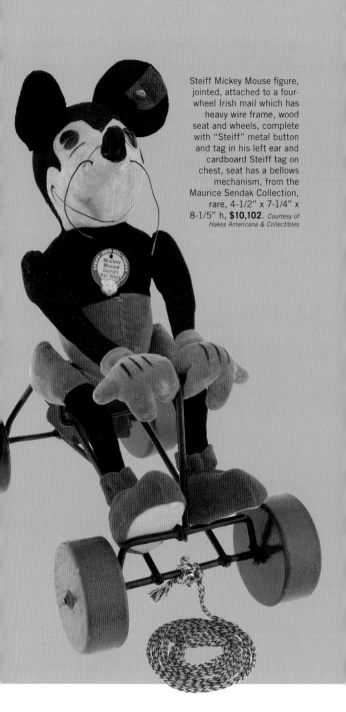

Steiff Mickey Mouse figure, jointed, attached to a four-wheel Irish mail which has heavy wire frame, wood seat and wheels, complete with "Steiff" metal button and tag in his left ear and cardboard Steiff tag on chest, seat has a bellows mechanism, from the Maurice Sendak Collection, rare, 4-1/2" x 7-1/4" x 8-1/5" h, **$10,102**. *Courtesy of Hakes Americana & Collectibles*

American Character Doll, 1952, Doll with Real Skin body, arms and legs and hard plastic head with sleep eyes, original girls outfit, functions as listed on box: cries tears, wets, blows bubbles, box end states, "I Love Lucy Baby" (doll was produced to capitalize on Lucy's pregnancy, hence this girl doll) scarce, doll is 14-3/4" h, box: 8-1/5" x 17" x 4-1/2" d, **$288.** *Hakes Americana & Collectibles*

Babby doll, America, African American child, circa 1920, made by Leo Moss, hand-sculpted paper mache with classic tears (Moss, of Macon, Georgia, was a handyman by trade and his folk dolls were created from the scraps of paper scraped from walls and made into a thick mache, then colored with boot dye, soot, or stove blacking as their base color), 26" h, **$7,500.** *Theriault's Antique Doll Auctions*

Doll, Germany, Kämmer & Reinhardt, 108, character doll, bisque head, painted blue/gray eyes with darker outer line to iris and red inner corner dot, auburn wig in two plaits with white ribbons, the eight ball jointed wood and composition body with swivel wrists and voice-box, incised K&R, 108, likely unique, 25-1/4" h, **$380,169**.

Doll, Germany, Kämmer and Reinhardt, "Karl," model 107, art character series, rare, **$42,000**.

Theriault's Antique Doll Auctions

Pair of dolls of Little Lulu with her purse in original box and a Buddy Lee wearing a Coca-Cola delivery uniform. Little Lulu: 14" h, Buddy Lee: 13" h, very good, **$850.50**.

Courtesy of James D. Julia Auctioneers, Fairfield, Maine, www.jamesdjulia.com

Dolls, Germany, pair, early 20th century, Kämmer and Reinhardt, marketed as 'Max and Moritz' comic strip character bisque head dolls and said to represent the Katzenjammer comic strip children, 16"h, **$50,000**. *Courtesy of Theriault's Antique Doll Auctions*

Double Bubble Ad Doll, great looking, large, early promotional advertising doll for Fleer Co.'s "Double Bubble" brand chewing gum, excellent, scarce, 21" x 9-1/25" x 4", **$460**.
Courtesy of William Morford Investment Grade Collectibles at Auction

Doll, Germany, circa 1860, paper mache, named "Hattie," owned by the Harriet Simonds of Franklinville, New York, died in 1863 at the age of 16 (to pass the time during her invalid years, she sewed for her doll, creating an extensive wardrobe of costumes and accessories), from the collection of Jean Strong, 12" h, **$8,750**. *Courtesy of Theriault's Antique Doll Auctions*

Doll, France, girl, circa 1884, bebe "H" by Halopeau, pressed bisque socket head original costume (blue velvet princess-style dress with braid and lace trim, undergarments, leather boots, earrings, fine silk bonnet), composition and wooden fully jointed body with straight wrists, from the family collection of Mildred Seeley, 19" h, **$40,000**. *Courtesy of Theriault's Antique Doll Auctions*

Doll, France, circa 1867, bisque wooden bodied poupee, from an original chateau estate in La Bourboule in the Auvergne region of central France, extensive original couturier trousseau with 14 gowns, ten bonnets, various blouses and jackets, coat, extensive undergarments, long train petticoats, small accwessories, and her original trunk which bears the shipping label from to Nantes La Bourboule on its side, **$36,000**. *Courtesy of Theriault's Antique Doll Auctions*

Doll, France, adult lady figure, circa 1850, porcelain, accompanied by an original trunk and trousseau, original hand-stitched couturiere costumes, bonnets, and accessories (considered a precursor to the classic French bisque poupee), 17" h, **$16,500**. *Courtesy of Theriault's Antique Doll Auctions*

Dolls, France, pair of children, French, circa 1914, bisque socket heads, character dolls by sculptor and illustrator Francisque Poulbot, Marks: SFBJ 239 Paris Poulbot (the dolls appeared in the Paris department store Etrennes catalogs of that year with the names Nenette and Rintintin, from the original drawings by Francisque Poulbot), 14" h, **$40,000**. *Courtesy of Theriault's Antique Doll Auctions*

Barbie

Debuting in aisles filled with baby dolls, Barbie was one of the first modern dolls to appear as a young adult (her first career was a "teenage fashion model"). The original 1959 doll was priced at $3. It is now in the permanent collections of the Smithsonian Institution and her persona was ranked #43 of the 2006 book "101 Most Influential People Who Never Lived." She remains the most popular doll in the world whose proportions are still causing controversy 55 years later, despite the fact her ever-changing careers positioned her as every bit as competent and capable as her male counterpart, Ken.

Fact:

Barbie was "born" in Germany. While traveling in Switzerland, creator Ruth Handler discovered an 11-1/2-inch German doll named Lilli, which was named after a popular comic strip character. Handler's company, Mattel, acquired the rights to the German doll and made modifications to create the original Barbie doll.

This pair of Barbie and Ken dolls are from the 1961 release. Ken has original, brunette flock hair and original red swim trunks, **$1,000-$1,500**/set, based on condition. *Courtesy Mattel - © 2012 Mattel, Inc. All Rights Reserved.*

1980 African American Barbie, No. 1293, **$20-$50**. *Courtesy Mattel - © 2012 Mattel, Inc. All Rights Reserved.*

Beautiful 1960s Barbie dolls, earliest side part American Girl on the original straight leg body and straight leg box and Ponytail Barbie with original curls and box. Both are all original and in fabulous new condition with no neck splits, no haircuts, and no nose nips or pinpricks, **$3,800** after 46 bids. *Photo courtesy valleygirlantiques*

1974 Barbie Town House playset #782, includes plastic furniture, some inflatable pieces, and white, baby grand piano, 3-1/2' h, **$30-$100** based on condition. *Courtesy Mattel - © 2012 Mattel, Inc. All Rights Reserved.*

Barbie's Little Sister Skipper doll (Mattel, 1963), excellent, original box, C7/C8, missing stand, with "Junior Edition Styles for Skipper, Skooter, and Ricky" pamphlet, **$150-$200**. *Heritage Auctions*

A 1978 Barbie Country Camper, 35" l, 13-1/2" h, 9-1/2" w, **$15-$45**, mint in box: **$80-$100**. *Courtesy Mattel - © 2012 Mattel, Inc. All Rights Reserved.*

CHAPTER 5

Toy Premiums

Pop quiz: What does a 5 carat diamond ring, a Tiffany Studios *Tulip* table lamp, and the world's largest collection of Cracker Jack premium toys have in common?

Each has sold at auction for $35,000.

The world's largest set of Cracker Jack premiums was assembled by Chad Dreier, CEO of the Fortune 500 company Ryland Homes from 1993 until 2009. Dreier was a collector of collections who set his sights on the promotional items dropped into boxes full of candied popcorn and peanuts. The collection of premiums was more than an odd pursuit. The result offered us a historical perspective on the genre and nature of American pop culture from the late 19th century to well into the 1990s.

We can thank the Fritz and Louis Rueckheim brothers and their partner, William Brinkmeyer, for perfecting Cracker Jack and its treasure-hunt marketing approach. The candy was around for nearly 20 years before the small "Toy Surprise" novelties appeared in 1912 and they were an instant hit with kids and even adults. Originally made of metal and paper, Cracker Jack premiums are plentiful and span several collecting genres (and three centuries!), which makes them easy to find and sell. The variety of novelties produced for the company is staggering: movie slide cards, dexterity puzzle, celluloid lamps, tops, tin soldiers, metal Baseball score counters and a tin litho horse and carriage are but a few of the earliest prizes.

Although the Drier Collection may have offered the largest collection of Cracker Jack premium toys, it did not include the original baseball cards the company slipped inside the boxes in 1914 and 1915. Collectors today have paid more than $101,575 for a single 1915 Cracker Jack Joe Jackson #103 card and $41,825 for a single 1914 card of Christy Mathewson. A complete set of

176 premium cards issued during these years sold for $31,070 at auction, a price rivaling the entire toy premium collection.

FOCUSED COLLECTIONS

Premium toys have a long and storied collecting history, partly because they span the greatest number of collecting categories. These toys were created for one reason – and one reason only: to increase publicity and sales of a particular product, service, or good. Marketers long realized the fast track to mom and dad's wallet was to appeal to children. The toys inspired brand loyalty and often gave the little tykes something to fiddle with while the adults could run errands or shop. As an effective and affordable form of advertising, the toys were distributed by the millions; however, their low cost and abundance did not contribute to their longevity, according to Scott Bruce, author of *Cereal Boxes and Prizes: 1960s*: "Flung into dumpsters by vengeful stock boys, store displays were the first to disappear. Cereal packages were burned in backyard blazes on top of dad's *Playboys*. Plastic gizmos, dug out of the box or mailed away, were heaved after little Joey choked on an Archie car wheel, Batman ring, or Seadog bo'sun whistle. Hoover-wielding Moms fed whatever escaped these purges to the holocaust of Spring Cleaning."[15] In the case of collectible toy premiums, survival sets values.

The extreme diversity makes it hard to classify all collecting categories here; however, collections are generally focused on one particular type of premium by origin:

Radio Toy Premiums: Hitting their peak in the 1930s and

---

15 *Cereal Boxes & Prizes: 1960s* is light on text, but a photo cavalcade of boxes and real-life premiums.

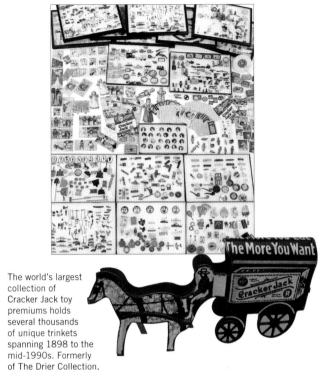

The world's largest collection of Cracker Jack toy premiums holds several thousands of unique trinkets spanning 1898 to the mid-1990s. Formerly of The Drier Collection, the massive collection includes 1898 Paper Dolls, (80+), pre-1910 Riddle Cards (17) Victorian Women pin backs, Cracker Jack Bears postcards sets (11) riddle books, baseball score counters, baseball spinner, water guns, various cast metal battleships, metal train cars and scores more. Among the items from the 1900s are movie slide cards, metal Baseball score counters, standing tin soldiers, spinning tops, storybooks, pot metal and celluloid lamps and trinkets, tin doll house serving trays, movie flip books, tin-litho horse and carriage, button mirrors, painted wooden boats, wood buildings and more. The collection also includes early, vintage Cracker Jack shipping crates and examples of various original packaging, **$35,000**.
Courtesy of Profiles In History

Ovaltine Radio Orphan Annie premium secret compartment brass decoder issued in 1936, excellent, 1-1/2" x 1-3/4", **$71**.
Courtesy of Heritage Auctions

1940s, an array of decoder pins, toy rings, special pinback buttons were issued to fans of "Little Orphan Annie," "Dick Tracy," "Captain Midnight," and "Lone Ranger" radio shows. Fans were required to send in labels, box tops, or lids as a proof of purchase in order to secure the toy, which boosted sales for the show's sponsors. Lincoln Logs produced a series of lead figures or "statuettes" as premiums for Libby's Evaporated Milk based on the "Og, Son of Fire" radio show in 1935. In the letter accompanying each figure, the milk company wrote, "Think how grand it will be to have all of them – standing in a line on your radio, or on the bureau or desk in your room! Listen carefully to the announcements following the 'Og, Son of Fire' programs ... telling you how you can get a statuette of Nada." Produced for only one year, each of the various character figures and two dinosaurs is now valued at about $50, making a set of seven worth roughly $350. Add the interactive toy map issued from the series ($350+) and the values surpasses $800. Thankfully, eBay has become a reliable source for entry-level radio premiums. But advanced collectors buy and sell through dedicated pop-culture auction houses such as Hake's Americana & Collectibles, hakes.com.

The highly sought after premiums are often paper goods. A 19-inch by 26-inch premium poster issued in the 1930s for Buck Rogers can bring $400 to $500 at auction. Careful: Reproductions exist and the originals were printed on matte-finish paper.

Advertising Toy Premiums: Toys were a powerful method for influencing consumers young and old. A 1974 mail-order kite for Jolly Green Giant peas sold for $125 on eBay and 15 bids pushed the end price of a 1960s Beatrice Foods Clark Bar Boy rubber squeeze toy to $107. The concept of the advertising toy goes back much farther, of course. The concept of sending in box tops and wrappers has its origin in the 1850s with Sweet Home Laundry Soap.

For the biggest bang for your buck, the market for automotive advertising toy premiums is deep and passionate. Mobil gas and other participating service stations offered a wide variety of tin litho scale model cars and trucks during the 1950s and 1960s. Sales pitches were issued directly to the children themselves, urging kids to "just get mom and dad to dive into our station today." Every 5-gallon purchase was tallied towards a 40-gallon total and a free tin truck made by Bandai of Japan. The 9-inch truck and an original (and ultra scarce) unused gas card sold for $173 at auction.

Cereal Box Prizes: My personal favorite was the Wacky Wallwalker, often found buried in the bottom of Kellogg's Apple Jacks cereal in the early 1980s. A rubber tacky surface allowed the octopus-looking critter to slowly "walk" down any vertical surface. More than 240 million were sold to my generation and it's hard to believe they now trade for $20+ in online auctions. Toys had been slipped into boxes well before the 1900s and collectors haven't yet given up the chase. For instance, a circa 1920 folded and tabbed tin Ford car, just 2-1/4 inches long, advertising Victor Toy Oats now sells for $77.

Although Kellogg's had premium-based marketing campaigns for decades, Ralston Cereals set the standard for more than 50 years. A standout in their red and white checkerboard boxes and later through licensed novelty brands, the prizes offered by the now defunct Ralston Cereals have a strong collecting base. Ralston offered a huge variety of premiums : a 1946 Tom Mix Look Around Premium toy ring will set you back $50; A circa 1950 Space Patrol Periscope (Only 25¢ When You Buy A Package Of Instant Or Regular Ralston) trades for $500; a 1992 "Urkel for President" pinback button from Urkelos cereal (based on the 1989-1997 sitcom *Family Matters*) runs $10.

Character Premiums: Many collectors specialize by character and it's easy to see why. Like today's app developers, food marketers were quick to capitalize on whatever concept or character held most children's appeal.[16] Superman currently holds the record for the most valuable single premium toy ever

---

16 For more examples on the impact of characters in branding, check out Chapter 2 of my *Picker's Pocket Guide: Signs* (Krause, 2014).

sold at auction. Hake's Americana & Collectibles sold a 1949 premium badge with its original leather wallet for $8,475 in 2011. A badge with a pin back brought $4,807 in November 2014. The badges were made by the Fo-Lee Gum Corp. of Philadelphia. The company launched Superman Bubble Gum in 1948 and it was a huge seller thanks to its tie-in with Columbia Pictures.

Badge premium, Superman, 1949 Fo-Lee Gum Corp., Philadelphia, die-cut shield badge with classic enamel paint image of Superman shown waist up breaking chest chains with his name in text at bottom coming out of circular border with enamel paint stars surrounded by brass luster burst design, another version has tabs on back to hold into the Superman premium wallet from Fo-Lee in 1949, excellent, 1-5/8" h, **$4,807**. *Courtesy of Hake's Americana & Collectibles*

PREMIUMS FADE

If you happen to notice the number of premiums available during the last 20 years, you're not alone. Lawsuits and low profits eliminated most toys. Even science has caused some controversy over the years by linking the toys to obese children. Research completed in 2012 showed that if premiums are offered in "healthier" McDonald's Happy Meals children were significantly more likely to pick those meals over unhealthy meals. Scientists showed policies that restrict toy premiums to food that meet nutritional criteria may promote healthier eating at fast-food restaurants.[17]

The cold, trans-fat truth to McDonald's Happy Meal premiums is that they are not valuable. The numbers of collectors who dabble in this area are now spending large amounts of money to acquire new items and those who are buying them spend about $1 a piece. It's easy to see why: most all the toys were mass produced, many survive because they did not have moving parts (which were costly to produce and would often break).

17 The Happy Meal Effect: The impact of toy premiums on healthy eating among children in Ontario, Canada. ncbi.nlm.nih.gov/pubmed/23618634.

Premium display, Superhero Fast Food Toy Display Group, circa 1990s-2000s, box lot of McDonald's Batman and other DC hero giveaway toy counter displays, including a ceiling mobile and a display of Looney Tunes Happy Meal toys with Bugs and the gang as DC heroes, fine to excellent, from the Ben Novack Jr. Estate Collection, **$17.** *Courtesy of Heritage Auctions*

Toy Skull Ring Group, circa 1960s, a group of seven vintage toy rings, likely from period vending machines, including one gold-colored metal ring, from the Jack and Julie Juka Collection, **$17.** *Courtesy of Heritage Auctions*

Figures, Pogo character vinyl figure group, 1969, Procter & Gamble, complete set of six figures: Pogo Possum, Albert Alligator, Beauregard Hound, Churchy La Femme, Howland Owl, and Porky Pine, excellent, 4" to 5" h, **$125.** *Courtesy of Heritage Auctions*

Tops, Cracker Jack premium, group of six different early tin litho Cracker Jack Co. product toy premium advertising tops, excellent, sizes range from 1-1/2" to 1-3/4" dia., **$150.**
Courtesy of William Morford Investment Grade Collectibles at Auction

Superman Contest Prize Ring, 1940, extremely scarce premium ring (aka the "Supermen of America Prize Ring"), this one was listed as the most valuable premium rings ever made, reportedly only 21 known, this ring was previously sold at a 1999 Sotheby's auction, very good, **$4,000-$7,000.** *Courtesy of Heritage Auctions*

Ring premium, issued circa 1950, Palmolive, depicting Clarabell the Clown character from Howdy Doody. One of five known to exist, ring is identical to Howdy version except on Clarabell's head is mounted a small brass hat fully 1/4" h, ring base, as on the Howdy version, shows two images of Clarabell with his elaborate collar and the brass loop to hold a battery has the same maker's name "Brownie Mfg. Co." along with "Pat. No. 2,516,180.," patent for "Finger Ring With Flashlight Adjustment" was filed in 1948 and granted July 25, 1950 to Meyer M. Brown (presumed owner of Brownie Mfg. Co.), painted facial details transforming the Howdy face into Clarabell, the hair is also totally different with just color accents, one of the Holy Grails of premium ring collecting, **$4,174.**

Courtesy of Hake's Americana & Collectibles

Captain America Badge, 1941, Marvel comic book premium, die-cut shield badge with his name and portrait above club name "Sentinels Of Liberty," badge came in either a copper or brass finish and this is the brass version, fine, 1-1/2" h, **$316.**

Courtesy of Hake's Americana & Collectibles

Car, Star Shoes premium, early die-cut tin litho advertising toy from "Star" brand shoes, featuring great image of early race car, excellent, 8-5/8" x 3-3/8" x 2-1/8", **$2,750**. *Courtesy of William Morford Investment Grade Collectibles at Auction*

Buck Rogers Badges premiums, 1935-57, set of three items: 1935 Cream of Wheat Whitehead & Hoag cello button (VG); rectangular 1952 Rocket Rangers Member tin tab (VF/NM); and 1957 round Satellite Pioneers litho tin tab (FN), rare, from the Don Vernon Collection, **$131**. *Courtesy of Heritage Auctions*

Car, Nash Advertising premium, early wooden advertising toy car give-away promoting John O'Hare, a Long Island City, NY, Nash car dealership, wooden body and moving wheels, with paper litho transfer car image on both sides, excellent, 2-3/8" x 5-3/8" x 3/4" w, **$242**.

Courtesy of William Morford Investment Grade Collectibles at Auction

Michael Thomasson set a world record in 2014 for assembling the world's largest video game collection as certified by Guinness World Records. He sold the 11,000-title collection in 2015 for a record sum. *Courtesy of Bianna Blank*

CHAPTER 6

Vintage Video Games

Still in its infancy, the collector market for vintage video games is by far the fastest-growing segment of today's vintage toy hobby. The relatively affordable prices for 95 percent of the consoles, cartridges, and accessories can be a misnomer to outsiders. Values hovering between $20 and $200 are both attracting new collectors and generating a sustainable supply of collectibles to meet new demand. If you could take a time machine to visit the early years of the more established toy collecting hobbies, you'd experience the same type of climate that dominates today's market for vintage video games.

"It's totally nostalgia," said Michael Thomasson, a video game designer, historian, and instructor of video game development. "I see these kids walking around with Nintendo T-shirts with pictures of controllers that read 'Know Your Roots' and 'Old School.' I look at Nintendo and see middle school – the second generation after the crash. Video games are in vogue now. When you start hitting 25 years old, you start reminiscing about simpler, happier times and a lot of those times involved video games for a lot of people."

Michael made international headlines in 2014 for selling his own vintage video game collection – the world's largest as certified by Guinness World Records. It was his third collection

Picker's Tip

Vintage video games may be the first toy collecting category in which quantity is pursued over quality. Since even games in poor cosmetic condition can still be played, building a large library of games may boost a collection's overall value.

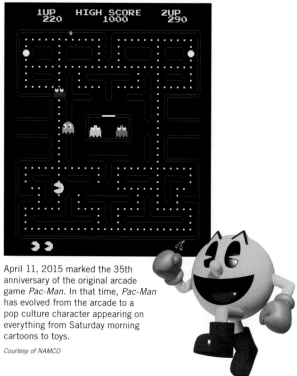

April 11, 2015 marked the 35th anniversary of the original arcade game *Pac-Man*. In that time, *Pac-Man* has evolved from the arcade to a pop culture character appearing on everything from Saturday morning cartoons to toys.

Courtesy of NAMCO

and included more than 11,000 titles with more than 2,600 of them were in their original shrink-wrapping. The games span more than 100 consoles and took nearly 30 years to complete, primarily because Michael took his time to buy low and sell high.

"I never pass up a bargain," he said. "I thought I was the only one doing this 20 years ago when I first started out – when the Game Boy Advance was getting phased out, I visited 17 game stores in a one-hour radius when they were all selling them for 'Buy 2 Get 2 Free.' The prices were 20 cents on the dollar and I was paying about $2.19 a game. I thought to myself, 'I know I can get that back someday.'"

The development of the internet and the arrival of eBay and lightning-fast communication between collectors changed everything – Michael realized he wasn't alone and that a whole community of game collectors existed in pockets around the country. Collectors have become more discerning and can be credited for encouraging mainstream culture to view games as art.

Michael Thomasson's Top 5 Collecting tips

The creator of the world's largest videogame collection reveals how you, too, can amass an amazing – and valuable – library of rare games and consoles:

PATIENCE: 80 percent of a new game's sales happen within two weeks of release. If you wait for at least a few months to pick up the game, you may be able to get it for 50 to 60 percent off.

PURSUIT: True collectors aren't above haunting garage sales, flea markets, online and estate sales. Even if you find duplicates, you can always resell them at a profit to feed your collection.

PART-TIME JOB: Consider getting a part-time job at a video game resale shop. Employees have the first opportunity to buy rare and unusual games when they are exchanged.

PLUGGED IN: Read lots of blogs, gaming news sites and industry gossip to learn which consoles are being phased out. A discontinued console or operating system usually means prices for those games are heading for a crash as most consumers move on. This crucial transition likely offers the lowest price these games will ever be.

PINT-SIZED: Indie developers make awesome games but poor distribution deals make quantities collectibles. Get familiar with video game publishers as well as those that have gone out of business. Remember: The largest video game companies hold more market share, making their games less likely to increase in value in the long run.

"The average age of a player is 27 to 35. Our next president could be a video game player. They are increasingly seen as art. Years ago the questions used to be 'Are movies art? Is photography art?' New technology doesn't get recognized for a couple of decades or generations later. Thankfully, it is the only medium that is larger than both the television and movie industries but you could talk with the original creators and founders," he said. "Our communication age makes it happen faster."

Interestingly, Michael predicts the gaming industry may struggle in the years to come. Now that developers have seen a taste of the profits a successful game can generate, companies are under more pressure to deliver huge profits. That expectation to set prices higher pushes some consoles and games out of the reach of families. "I see it struggling in the near future because of the dynamic of the game blockbuster," Michael said.

"It's hard for a family to pay $400 for a console and another $65 for a game. They are being challenged by inexpensive games such as *Minecraft*.

Picker's Tip

More than 100,000 *Pac-Man* arcade cabinets were sold in 1980.

Angry Birds was inexpensive to make, but *Destiny* (Activision, 2014) took half a billion dollars.[18] It took 20,000 people and it will be a 10-year franchise and there will be a lot of profit from it, but it just doesn't have the originality you see on the Indie scene."

Collectors put a premium on originality and novelty – even if the game isn't immediately a commercial success. The demand underscores David Kaelin's business plan for Austin, Texas-based Game Over Videogames, an independent chain of classic and used video game stores, gameovervideogames.com. Capping three years of growth at 276 percent, the chain opened its 11th location and was ranked on *Inc. Magazine*'s 5,000 fastest-growing private companies in America in 2014. The company offers more than 10,000 games, systems, and accessories per store for Atari 2600, Intellivision, NES, SNES, Genesis, Dreamcast, Playstation, Saturn, 3DO, Turbografx-16 and more. In 2013, the company saw gross sales hit $2.1 million.

"Collecting has definitely gone main stream," David said. "This is a very wide market and just like the rare coin and stamp market, we see it going in that direction. Eventually people will be buying these games to invest – just to buy and stick it in a closet for 20 years to double its worth."

The majority of Game Over Videogame's customers are those who play games – or haven't played in a while – and may be going through a nostalgia phase and want to play the classic games again, David said. With their own children in tow, adults are eager to share the personal relationship they had with games popular 20 or 25 years ago when they were a teenager.

David sees commonalities among customers of similar age

---

18 Activision CEO Bobby Kotick claimed the company invested $500 million in *Destiny* including development, marketing, and other costs, but backpedaled on that claim a few months later.

David Kaelin of Game Over Videogames. *Courtesy of Game Over Videogames*

groups: "The mind sets root in the gaming institution popular at the time. If you were in your teens in the 1970s, it's Atari. A teen in the 1980s? Then you're into Nintendo."

Customers are now in their mid-30s and early 40s and are rapidly gaining the disposable income needed to buy vintage games. "Males still make up the majority and it's a problem that more women aren't involved in the game community, but 30 to 40 percent of players are women. In terms of our customers, the largest customer group is adult males and second is adult females ... and then kids."

David said the appeal of the most sought after vintage games is two-fold:

- Classic titles offer a unique gaming experience that is family-friendly, innovative, and challenging.
- The cost of the vintage games is far less than the cost of cutting-edge releases.

"I've been in this business 10 years now and in the beginning, the only retro games that people were looking for were Atari or NES (Nintendo Entertainment System)," he said. "Over time that changed and now covers Super Nintendo, then Nintendo 64, and soon Game Cube, partly because of the release of *Smash Bros.* for Nintendo Wii."

An early arcade video game promo by Atari for *Space Invaders*, pinback, circa 1980, Atari premium, with metal back and bar pin, button was likely released in 1980 to promote the release of *Space Invaders* on the Atari 2600 game system at that time, scarce and historic promotional button from the era which saw the video game industry expand from a novelty to a global business, 2-1/4", **$105**. *Courtesy of Hake's Americana & Collectibles*

MAINSTREAM SALES + COLLECTOR DEMAND

The market for vintage games may be just starting out, but it is uniquely – and simultaneously – establishing itself as a cornerstone on both retailer's shelves and collector's cabinets. The Toy Industry Association proclaimed youth electronics as the fastest growing toy category in 2013. The category includes video games and hand-held toys and charted an astounding 32 percent boost over 2012.[19]

Rare vintage games can now bring five figures at auctions. In 2012, a copy of *Air Raid* for the Atari 2600 sold for $33,433. The boxed version was only the third version of the game ever discovered and the only one that retained its original instruction manual. A year later, a copy of the Nintendo Entertainment System game *Family Fun Fitness: Stadium Events* was discovered at a North Carolina Goodwill thrift store. The game was picked up for a $1 and later sold for $12,000. The game, which was originally released on July 1, 1987, has popped up again at auction for as much as $38,000.

At the top of the common market reside arcade games, the cabinet monitor combos that once occupied the corners of every pizza parlor in the country during the 1970s and 1980s. Average arcade games in working condition sell for $400 to $500. More iconic arcade games, such as *Asteroids*, *Pac-Man*, and *Pole Position*, easily command $500 to $600.

A company called Video Game Authority has stepped in as a third-party independent grader which cases games, just as other authorities case comic books, coins, and sports cards. The service offers a standard grading scale for sealed games, systems, and accessories (from mainstream platforms) and a custom grade for non-standard , deluxe and special edition games.

---

19 Toy Industry Association annual statement.

Extreme Hunting video game, Sammy, 2000, **$1,400**.

Courtesy of Premier Props

Countertop video game by Tatio, dated 2005, contains ten games including *Space Invaders, Jungle Hunt*, etc. Original shipping box, minor rust to case, not tested, 25" h x 23" d x 17-1/2" w, **$130** + 18%.
Courtesy of Mosby & Co

The Atari Model CX-2600 video game console was Atari's most successful endeavor. This set includes the original controllers and cartridges including three joystick controllers, two paddle controllers, and a hella stack of games including *Spider Fighter, Combat, River Raid, Pitfall!, Tac-Scan, Breakout, Oink!, Star Ship, Enduro, Riddle of the Sphinx, Journey Escape, Vanguard, Yars' Revenge, Berzerk, Megmania, Mouse Trap, Frogger, Starmaster, Dragster, Pac-Man*. A collection like this can still be found for under **$100**. *Courtesy of Leonard Auctioneers*

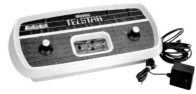

This is Coleco's first video game console, circa 1976. It plays tennis, hockey and handball. This great piece of gaming history sold for **$30** at auction.
Courtesy of Nette Auctions

MOST VALUABLE VINTAGE VIDEO GAME CONSOLES

Collectors are an odd sort – they eschew the mainstream and cherish the oddballs. Here's a list of the most valuable consoles sought after by collectors.

NINTENDO GAME BOY LIGHT
TEZUKA OSAMU LIMITED EDITION

A 1998 limited edition transparent handheld honoring cartoonist Osamu Tezuka, creator of *Astro Boy*, *Black Jack* and *Jungle Emperor* only released in Japan, much to the chagrin of the rest of the world.

SOLD: $420 ON EBAY

SPECIAL EDITION PIKACHU
NINTENDO 64 CONSOLE

A 2000 Toys R' Us exclusive, features a Pokemon ball for the power switch and the character Pikachu on the game surface – complete with light-up cheeks!

SOLD: $799 ON EBAY

MICROSOFT TACO BELL
XBOX 360 SLIM

The only way to win this purple Taco Bell-themed Microsoft Xbox 360 was to be one of the lucky 30 Canadians in the world who scored an instant win code. Thankfully for collectors, one of the winners decided to sell their console in late 2014. The campaign lasted from July to September 2012.

SOLD: $532 ON EBAY

SONY PLAYSTATION 4 20TH ANNIVERSARY CONSOLE PS4 LIMITED EDITION SEALED

Sony created 12,300 20th anniversary Playstation 4 consoles designed to commemorate the first gray Playstation released in December 1994.

SOLD: $20,100 ON EBAY

SONIC 10TH ANNIVERSARY SEGA DREAMCAST CONSOLE

In addition to being one of 40 Sega Dreamcast consoles ever made to commemorate the 10th anniversary of its Sonic the Hedgehog game, the consoles were personally signed by video game designer Yuji Naka.

SOLD: $2,518 ON EBAY

S.T.A.R.S LIMITED EDITION SEGA DREAMCAST

One of just 200 ever made, the S.T.A.R.S Limited Edition Sega Dreamcast was only released in Japan. The rare consoles were only distributed in 2000 by Sega via Dreamcast Direct, the company's own gaming group, and through Famitsu, a Japanese gaming magazine.

SOLD: $2,291 ON EBAY

Console, Nintendo GameCube System, with all hookups, one controller, 128 MB card, **$25-$75**, depending on accessories, edition, and condition. *Courtesy of Sabertooth Auctions, LiveAuctioneers*

Commemorative premium, crystal orb, 1990, Nintendo, given as part the "Nintendo Power Final Fantasy Treasure Quest" contest announced in the Sept./Oct. 1990 issue of the *Nintendo Power* video game magazine, noted as second prize was one of 50 custom-crafted crystal orbs embossed with the *Final Fantasy* name/emblem, clear crystal came with a "Kusak Cut Glass Works" box and has a flattened bottom with the *Final Fantasy* name and emblem reverse etched into it; when viewed from above, the orb magnifies the design for a nice display, 3-1/4" dia, **$1,391**.

Courtesy of Hake's Americana & Collectibles

The Nintendo Game Boy was released in 1989 with a monochromatic body and stereo sound. Early versions trade for **$10** to **$50** depending on accessories.

Courtesy of Courtesy of Nintendo

Handheld, 2013, Gold Nintendo 3DS XL Limited Edition, decorated with Triforce logo, with download of complete *Legend of Zelda Link Between Worlds* game, **$250-$300**.
Courtesy of eBay

Video game cartridge, *Super Dodge Ball Cart*, 1989, CSG Imagesoft, Nintendo, **$15-$20**.
Courtesy of eBay

Video game cartridge, *The Flintstones: The Rescue of Dino and Hoppy*, 1991, Nintendo, **$15-$25**. *Courtesy of eBay*

Console, ColecoVision, 1982, home video game console, with accessories and *Donkey Kong* cartridge game, MIB, **$300-$500**.
Courtesy of eBay

Console, Nintendo Entertainment System, Control Deck, 1988, MIB with accessories sealed in original packaging, **$400-$500**.
Courtesy of eBay

Handheld games lot, group includes nine vintage handheld video games: (2) 1982 pocketsize *Nintendo Donkey Kong* multi-screen game and watch; both are in original boxes; (3) *Long Bomb Football* games; *Speed Freak* handheld game in original box; handheld *Dungeons & Dragons* game in original box, *Sub Chase* game in working condition; *Missile Invader* game in working condition (also included is an original vintage Rubik's Cube), **$513**.
Courtesy of Affiliated Auctions

Action Figure Prototype, GI Joe, 1964, original sculpt by Hasbro Creative Director Don Levine, plastic body with wire-spring joints, and a hand-painted plastic head that was created by pulling a temporary mold from a carved wooden original (still the world record for the most valuable action figure ever sold at auction), 12" h, **$200,001**.
Courtesy of Heritage Auctions

CHAPTER 7

Action Figures

Kevin Stark is a creator of childhood.

As a freelance artist, Kevin was part of the team to design the now famous *Teenage Mutant Ninja Turtle* toy line in 1990. Based on the comic books of the same name, the toys were recently acknowledged as *the* hottest toy for the holidays that year. In fact, I received a full set that year and happily passed them onto my son 15 years later. The original retail price was $5.95, an almost quaint amount when you consider a lot of six original figures now brings $200 or better at auction.

Kevin Stark, toy designer and founder of the Toy & Action Figure Museum, of Pauls Valley, OK.
Courtesy of Eric Bradley

Kevin branched out to design action figures for *Toxic Crusaders, The Mask, The Simpsons,* Stretch Armstrong, and even Universal Studio's *The Mummy* line. In 2005, he launched the Toy & Action Figure Museum in his hometown of Pauls Valley, Oklahoma, the only museum of its kind in the world.

Packed wall to wall with figures, rotating exhibits give credit to character creators and toy makers from concept to creation and feature a "figure shrine" worthy of the Metropolitan Museum of Art. The tens of thousands of figures in Kevin's archive pay homage to both popular retail lines such as Mego and LJN Toys to custom figures and limited edition sculpts by named artists.

Kevin said the relatively recent development of collectible figures for adults made small-run figures profitable for manufacturers and fun for collectors to pursue. "Instead of having to design a piece to sell 40,000 figures, you can create a much more detailed figure priced at $140 and only have to sell 1,200 figures."

The limited production runs have a tradition of stoking collector demand, which increases values over the long run. "But that fact also gets the collector to pay all that much up front

Picker's Tip

Even loose action figures are collectible and valuable. Don't pass them up if you see them at a flea market or garage sale since many collectors buy lesser-quality toys to serve as place holders until they can afford better versions.

because they know if you don't get it when it comes out then you'll have to spend more in the secondary market."

Kevin calls the 1990s the Golden Age of Action Figures, and toys from that era are starting to rapidly increase in value. "You went from little to no superheroes to nothing but superheroes," he says. "I was a child of the 1960s and a lot of what happened in the 1990s was the result of people like me who grew up without affordable toys – we wanted better."

Displays at the Toy & Action Figure Museum celebrate the art and design of the modern action figure, including these various examples from DC Comics. *Courtesy of Eric Bradley*

The king of the modern collectible toy movement was Todd McFarlane, the cartoonist and toy designer. "He upped the ante, so to speak," Kevin said. The age guidelines on these toys are less about choking hazards and more about being old enough to manage psychological trauma.

By following pop culture trends, collectors and sellers can zero in on toys that have the potential to increase in value over time. In October 2014, the mega toy seller Toys "R" Us pulled MEZCo's action figures from the drug and violence-fueled AMC cable series, *Breaking Bad*.[20] The packages were sold in the store's adult action figure area, but were pulled after complaints that the toys glorified drug abuse. The tiny little bags of cash and methamphetamine didn't help, but the move did make the toys more collectible. On shelves, the six-inch toys retailed for $20.99 apiece. The figures now sell for as much as $229 on eBay – a ten-fold increase. I'm not too convinced those prices will remain high into the distant future, however, only because the television show has a cult status only enjoyed by adults. Traditionally lines

20 Toys "R" Us Pulls *Breaking Bad* Action Figures After Petition, nbcnews.com.

A massive collection of vintage and modern action figures on display at the Toy & Action Figure Museum. *Courtesy of Eric Bradley*

that appeal to children ages 8 to 13 are the ones to increase in value for 40 or 50 years, but the modern action figure market has a way of demolishing such traditions.

It's difficult to find exact figures, but the number of brick and mortar stores that exclusively sell vintage action figures has replaced the traditional sellers of tin and antique toys. The same is true with toy shows and conventions; events featuring vintage and contemporary toys are held more frequently. This shift comes in lockstep with changing demographics but also signals a shift in pop culture: although it may start in childhood, collecting action figures is a socially acceptable hobby for adults, too.

Today's action figure collectors are much more discerning and pay attention to details – a relatively new development that is pushing collector prices higher, said collector and hobby seller Scott Walker, who specializes in selling action figures from Marvel Legends line. The Marvel Legends action figure series, which was first manufactured by Toy Biz (2002-2006) and then by Hasbro (2007-2014), offers a perfect example of

Toy Biz's 2003 Thor figure, left, is often found priced from **$40 to $60 each**. Hasbro's 2007 Thor, right, is often found priced from **$30 to $40**.

Courtesy of Eric Bradley

how the collector's eye influences values. Here's a look at how the two companies issued figures of Thor:

Toy Biz's 2003 figure was produced in Series three. It weighs 1.8 pounds, features extensive painted and shaded detailing, has 31 points of articulation, and came with a custom stand and comic book. It is often found priced from $40 to as much as $60 each.

Hasbro's 2007 take on Thor was produced in Series 17. It weighs 15.2 ounces, is hollow, and the only coloration comes

Scott Walker.
Courtesy of Eric Bradley

from the molded plastic. With just eight points of articulation, the toy came with a "builder piece" to assemble a complete figure of the character Blob. It is often found priced from $30 to $40.

"The Toy Biz version is well built," Scott said. "It's got the level of detail collectors seek out and are willing to pay more for. It originally sold for $10. The Hasbro version lost a lot of creativity and detail and a lot of the quality ... and was sold for $20."

Scott said his most popular figures are those for the cult character Deadpool. He can't keep the version made by Toy Biz in stock when it's priced at $200 or less. Lucky for him, he bought a case of them when they debuted for about $8 a piece.

"He is by far the No. 1 most collected figure by Toy Biz," he said. "I make it a point to watch trends and price my figures based on the cost for the customer to find the same toy. I price it taking into consideration the travel and shipping and other costs they will have to pay." Sure enough, a quick check on most toy sites and online auctions show the figure is a brisk seller for $200 to $240.

Scott's advice? "Take the time to really know what you want

Jose, left, and Bernard Flores, 10, buy and sell vintage action figures to fund Bernard's hobby of collecting vintage *Star Wars* characters. The two have an active eBay business, which they manage from their smartphones.

Courtesy of Eric Bradley

– narrow it down," he said. "Take the time to research and know the price you want to pay." Scott spends a lot of time checking the latest Completed Listings results on eBay and current prices on Amazon. With this data in mind, he also makes note of values in his own local market and then sets a price based on the two (as well as his costs, of course). "You want to pay attention to what collectors are doing and what retailers are doing."

You'd think all this wheeling and dealing would be reserved strictly to adults, and that may be the case with other collectible toy categories. Not so with action figures, and Bernard Flores is living proof. At just 10 years old, the kid rattles off facts on the defunct Kenner Products like he's reciting a Christmas list.

"Kenner was started in 1947 and Hasbro closed it in 2000," he said of the company that produced his favorite toys of all: vintage *Star Wars* action figures. He also collects *Ghostbuster* action figures and Teenage Mutant Ninja Turtles. Bernard started collecting about two years ago and has spent hours on YouTube.com learning about figures. A few months later, he dragged his dad with him to flea markets to find new additions to his collection. He started buying action figures from other lines to resell to fund his hobby. "I told my dad the older figures are cool, but about that time I learned that not everything that's old is valuable," he said.

Bernard finds the toys and even haggles for a deal. Their No. 1 rule is to at least double their money on every purchase and pick up duplicates whenever possible. Besides setting up at small toy shows, the father-son team sells figures on eBay through the site's mobile smartphone app.

"We list them through our phones," Bernard's dad, Juan, said. "It's very easy to just take a picture and list it." The two can sell between $100 and $500 a month through the app. With nearly 300,000 action figures listed on eBay at any given time – yes, 300,000 – the success they've achieved from weekends shopping at flea markets gives some perspective in how much money is trading hands.

STAR WARS RULES IT ALL

It's because of *Star Wars* collectors like Bernard that Kyle O'Neil remains focused on his niche resale business. For the last eight years, Kyle has been known as a Ripper, one of the very few who specializes in only the accessories (guns, helmets, swords, etc) originally sold with the figures. "These smaller

Kyle O'Neil.
Courtesy of Eric Bradley

weapons are the first things to get lost when a figure is opened," Kyle said. "I focus on the *Star Wars* made from 2000 to 2012 – I really gravitate to that decade and I think with another wave of movies coming out, the movies released in that decade will be seen as 'vintage' and interest will grow for their figures as well."

One of Lewis' largest customers is the hobby customizers, collectors who repaint figures to follow story lines in *Star Wars* novelizations or their own vision for the character's universe. It took him more than a year to assemble enough to cover a six-foot table at a recent 50-vendor North Dallas Toy Show. He offered a table full of weapons and assorted vehicles, including furniture sections from the famous cantina scene in the original *Star Wars* and Jedi council seats first seen in *Star Wars Episode I: The Phantom Menace.*

Lewis and Bernard are the yin and the yang of *Star Wars* collectors – both seek new additions to their collections and come together thanks to some ingenuity and profit making. Both find interest in the action figure hobby and find a way to profit from it as well.

Picker's Tip

Collectors of larger scale figures gravitate towards IKEA's DETOLF lighted glass-door cabinet to display collections and sets.

Action figures and retail stand, 1965, 12-figure set of original James Bond action figures accompanied by counter top display stand, including No. 1 James Bond with Deadly Baretta Pistol, No. 2 James Bond (Blue Shirt) with Hi-Power Scope Rifle, No. 3 James Bond in Scuba Outfit with Spear gun (blister has crack), (3 copies) No. 4 Odd Job with Dangerous Derby, No. 5 "M" Bond's Brilliant Boss, No. 6 Goldfinger-Bond's Cruel Adversary, No. 7 Moneypenny Loyal Gal-Friday, No. 8 Largo-Cruel One Eyed Villain, No. 9 Domino-She Lives With Danger and No. 10 Dr. No with Poison Vial, also included are (3) large blister packs including Secret Agent Gun Case and Bullet-Shield "M"s Desk and the blister pack Spin-top Pool Table and Deadly Laser Ray as well as the Dr. No's Dragon Tank and Largo's Hydrofoil Yacht, 30-1/2" h x 19" w x 10" d. It can be found for between **$700 and $1,000.** *Courtesy of Heritage Auctions*

Action figure, 1974, MEGO, Iron Man, type 1, original box with 25 cent price tag, mint in box, 8" h, **$200-$250.**

Courtesy of Hake's Americana & Collectibles

GI JOE — THE GRANDDADDY OF ALL ACTION FIGURES

The history of GI Joe – considered the granddaddy of action figures – is well documented. Based on an original idea from Stan Weston, Hasbro Creative Director Don Levine created the first prototype in 1964, as a testosterone response to Barbie's debut just five years earlier. Values for loose figures without original boxes are slipping, but figures retaining clothes and the original box have regularly sold for $300-$400 or more at auction in recent years. Collectors are hungry for original accessories from the 1964 line of carded uniforms, helmets, scuba tanks and skis. These sets quickly trade at $50 to $150 each, depending on rarity.

Action figure, GI Joe, 1964, #7500, Hasbro, painted hair, all original in box with field manual, 11-1/2" h, **$300-$400**. *Courtesy of LiveAuctioneers*

Action Figure, GI Joe, 1964, Action Marine with box, highly sought-after Marine C9 figure, complete with booklet and equipment, battle scene, and club brochures, plus boot removal instruction page and folded one-page catalog, from the Jack and Julie Juka Collection, 12" h, **$191**. *Courtesy of Heritage Auctions*

Action figure, GI Joe, 1967, Hasbro, Deep Freeze figure, complete with waffle boots, snow shoes, sled, fur coat and ice pick hammer, loose, from the Jack and Julie Juka Collection, 12" h, **$150-$200**. *Courtesy of Heritage Auctions*

Action figure, GI Joe, 1967, Hasbro, Sailor figure with sea rescue outfit, including life vest, helmet, binoculars, flag, and duffle bag, and coveted original box, figure and accessories, from the Jack and Julie Juka Collection, 12" h, **$334**. *Courtesy of Heritage Auctions*

TOY CASE STUDY: CUSTOM ENVIRONMENTS

Licensed, high-end action figures are some of the first to increase in value. Sophisticated sculpts, limited production runs, and larger scale appeal to adults who are also fans of the sci-fi and fantasy movies that inspire the figures.

A growing off-shoot of this hobby is design firms that make coveted custom, true-to-screen environments based on pivotal scenes in movies that transcend into pop culture touchstones. The Upper Michigan firm XCES Studios makes such environments, which have increased in value as a collectible compliment to any 1:6 scale figure; however, it has most often seen use with Hot Toys' Batman and Joker figures from the second installment in director Christopher Nolan's *Dark Knight* trilogy.

The hand-painted Military Police Interrogation Room environment (MPIRE 003) features a two-way mirror and the furnishings (MPIRE 004) include a table, chairs and a working LED lamp. Just 100 sets were made. There's also a Jail Cell environment. The sets accommodate any 1/6 scale figures. If you can locate all the sets and figures, they will now cost between $1,250 and $1,500, on average, depending on the figures you buy to compliment the sets. Not a bad return on accessories and figure that originally cost roughly $850.

"The MPIRE 004 accessory set was originally $89.99 and the MPIRE 003 Interrogation Room was $249.99," said Tyson Butorac, owner of XCES Studios. "We have filled all orders to date, and have sold out our full stock of the complete MPIRE 004 accessory sets (the table, chairs, and LED lamp). It's been an absolutely fantastic experience and I'm enjoying every minute of creating and designing new realistic dioramas for fellow collectors."

The Military Police Interrogation Room (MPIRE 003) was made famous in *The Dark Knight* starring Christian Bale and Heath Ledger. The sophisticated set features a two-way mirror.

XCES Studio's Military Police Interrogation Room Accessory Pack (MPIRE 004) includes a table, two chairs, and working LED lamp.

Theater playset, 1966, Ideal Toy Corp, Batman Puppet Theatre Playset, Sears-exclusive set, three plastic-head hand puppets, Batman, Robin, and the Joker, from the Ben Novack, Jr. Estate Collection, rare, **$2,270**. *Courtesy of Heritage Auctions*

Action figures, contemporary, Batman and Robin Serial Action Figure Group, unauthorized set of customized 8" action figures modeled after Robert Lowery (the Batman) and Johnny Duncan (Robin), stars of the Columbia Pictures 1949 15-chapter serial, from the Ben Novack Jr. Estate Collection, **$100**. *Courtesy of Heritage Auctions*

Action figures, circa 1970s, set containing all jointed blow molded plastic figures of Batman and Robin produced in Argentina by Piola, NPP, Inc. marking, figures are mint as packaged, fine, figures 10" and 9" h, **$3,921**.

Courtesy of Hake's Americana & Collectibles

Action figures, 1982-1985, Mattel, set of four, including "Evil Warrior" figures - "Evil & Sees Everything" Tri-Klops and "Evil Master Of Odors" Stinkor, as well as "Heroic Warrior" and "Heroic Spy & Master Of Camouflage" Moss Man and the evil King Hiss, "Dreadful Disguised Leader Of The Snake Men," mint in box, **$151.**

Courtesy of Hake's Americana & Collectibles

Action figures, 1984-89, Kenner, Super Powers Action Figure Group, unopened blister-packs, including Aquaman (with mini comic book); Batman; Golden Pharaoh; Kalibak (with mini comic); Red Tornado (with mini comic)' and Robin. In addition, there is a Super Amigos Superman from Argentina, **$100-$200 set.** *Courtesy of Heritage Auctions*

Action figures, 1967, Ideal, Captain Action Green Hornet Uniform Set, original packaging, the set was released at the very tail-end of the second wave of uniform sets and had poor distribution in some areas, **$3,600**.

Courtesy of Heritage Auctions

Action figures, MEGO Toy Group, 1970s, group of 39 carded DC and Marvel action figures, plus a boxed Joker Mobile, from the Ben Novack, Jr. Estate Collection, **$1,553**. *Courtesy of Heritage Auctions*

Action figures, 1988, Playmates, group of six of Leonardo, Donatello, Raphael, Michaelangelo, Splinter and April O'Neal (later release with yellow jumpsuit with orange accents). April notwithstanding, all figures are from first series of Ninja Turtle action figures released by Playmates, ©1988 Mirage Studios, mint as packaged, figures: 4-1/4" to 4-1/5" h, **$100-$200**. *Courtesy of Hake's Americana & Collectibles*

Action figures, 1989, Playmates, group of six villains: Shredder, Bebop, Rocksteady, Foot Soldier, Krang and Baxter Stockman. Excluding Krang and Baxter Stockman, mint as packaged, figures: 4-1/4" to 5" h, **$200-$300**. *Courtesy of Hake's Americana & Collectibles*

Action figure prototype resin cast, 1987, Playmates, Michaelangelo from T*eenage Mutant Ninja Turtles*, plaster prototype resin cast from the collection of co-creator Kevin Eastman, **$2,151**.

Courtesy of Heritage Auctions

Action playset, 1977, Kenner, Star Wars Cantina Adventure playset plus four action figures of bounty hunters Greedo, Hammerhead, Snaggle Tooth and Walrus Man, rare, fine, 14" x 18" x 1-1/2" d, **$584**. *Courtesy of Hake's Americana & Collectibles*

Return of the Jedi (20th Century Fox, 1983) Kenner Jabba the Hutt Action Playset with original box, complete with "Salacious Crumb" on a slave rope, Jabba, action figures on the left of the photo on the box, were sold separately, 8" x 8" x 13-1/2", **$200-$300**.
Courtesy of Heritage Auctions

Action figure, 1977, Kenner, Princess Leia, 12-card back, original vinyl cape, mint as packaged 3-3/4" h, **$350-$400**.

Courtesy of Hake's Americana & Collectibles

◀ Poster, 2003, promoting Boba Fett action figure, Hasbro, from Star Wars Unleashed series, 30" x 40", **$41**.

Heritage Auctions

▶ Action figure, 1977, Kenner, R2-D2, blister card contains figure, mint as packaged, 2-1/4" h, **$300-$400**.

Courtesy of Hake's Americana & Collectibles

◀ Action figure, 1977, Kenner, C-3PO, blister card contains figure, mint as packaged, 3-3/4" h, **$300-$400**.

Courtesy of Hake's Americana & Collectibles

▶ Action figure, 1977, Kenner, blister card contains figure which was produced with either a vinyl cape or fabric robe; this is fabric robe version, mint as packaged, 2-3/8" h, **$300-$400**.

Courtesy of Hake's Americana & Collectibles

The *LEGO Movie* and *The LEGO Movie* product range introduced some of the most popular LEGO figures as well as several new characters, allowing fans of various generations to jointly experience the LEGO world as never seen before. Set #70809, **$100-$150**.

Used by permission.® 2014 The LEGO Group

CHAPTER 8

LEGO Sets

Thankfully for collectors, the history of LEGO is well documented. Many sets still survive from the company's boon time following the development of the LEGO Mursten, aka LEGO brick, in 1949. Sales didn't reach the United States until 1961, but by the end of the decade, annual sales topped 18 million sets composed of bricks made from 218 different shapes. It's hard to believe that LEGO System will celebrate its 60th anniversary in 2015.

LEGO Building Systems were originally designed for child collectors. The LEGO System ensured that every piece could be interconnected with one another. The first organized set was called Town Plan No. 1 and it included a hotel, various buildings, and even an Esso gas station.

Interestingly, the market for loose vintage bricks is, so far, practically nonexistent. Sacks of the familiar red, blue, and white original colors go unsold at public auctions: without original boxes or instructions, the bricks are practically anonymous. Building sets sold from the late 1970s through the late 1990s - prior to the licensing revolution that transformed the company during the 2000s - often trade on today's market for $25 to as much as $300 depending on condition of the original box and completeness. The key here is the existence of the original box. Take set 422, the classic LEGO Space Shuttle. True to collector's fascination with everything relating to outer space, LEGO spaceship building sets command a premium. The set in its original box trades for $225; however, without the box and instructions, the

Picker's Tip

The first LEGO bricks were made in 1949 of cellulose acetate and had slits on the side to allow builders to add windows or doors; the modern interlocking brick was patented in 1958. Sets from the 1950s most often appear at auction in Denmark or Germany and sell for **$400-$600** USD.

set is deemed no different than any other group of bricks.

LEGO has publicly avoided commenting on the secondary collector market for its sets and figures, which it brands as "minifigures" or "minifigs." That hasn't stopped the company from identifying some sets as "hard to find" and "retired," which surely increases demand for them in the long run whether LEGO gets a cut or not. In early 2015 on its own ecommerce site, LEGO promoted 55 sets tagged as "hard to find," with many of them marked "Sold Out." This subtle tracking of supply and demand can be interpreted as LEGO's tacit approval of the active collector market and perhaps even a bellwether of future collectability.

COLLECTOR'S PARADISE

Today's collector market for LEGO sets is absolutely on the climb, says Anthony Bearden, owner of Minifigs, Bricks and More of Denton, Texas. The shop is one of the dozens of independent toy companies that have opened across the county in recent years to meet the demand of LEGO collectors seeking to trade and collect vintage sets. The store is a hub of activity, with young adults making up the largest customer base.

"There is definitely a large group of collectors who are interested in buying sets and preserving them, keeping it in their original packaging to store it," he said. "All of the vintage or retired sets we carry are at least doubled the manufacturer's suggested retail price." Take the hard-to-find Fire Brigade, #10197. The realistic 1930s fire station set was retired in 2009 and retailed for $150, but now trades for $315.

Sets like Fire Brigade harkens back to LEGO's first 20 years, when it was developing building systems based on town plans. For decades, the company established itself as the de facto leader in toy building blocks, but designs did not inspire today's collecting fervor. I remember receiving LEGO sets for years through the 1980s at Christmas but, like I suspect many kids did at that time, I put the set on my dresser to look at and it was eventually tossed into a toy box. In other words, the sets were kinda boring. Clearly the appeal wasn't there: by 1998, the company had reported its first deficit. It's an important turning point in the company's history, which necessitated a revolution that changed everything: licensing.

LICENSING REVOLUTION

No other LEGO building sets are as heavily traded and command better prices than its licensed theme sets. Star Wars! Harry Potter! Spider-Man! Batman! SpongeBob! The licensing revolution that arrived in 1999 not only jump-started global sales, it also jump-started an aftermarket that fueled demand for the next great set to come.

It's important to note the licensing sets arrived just as the internet was establishing itself as a crucial tool for collectors. The web is now home to several sites devoted to LEGO collectors. Sites such as BrickPicker.com, BrickSet.com, BrickLink.com, and ThePlasticBrick.com are but a few that now create a community of collectors. On BrickLink.com, more than 612,000 sets are for sale as are more than 23 million (yes, million) parts and 1.4 million minifigs. It's a veritable museum of LEGO, with sets sorted by year and category. *Star Wars* sets dominate the set listings, followed by 13 series of minifigures releases from 2010 to the present.

FUTURE COLLECTIBLES

It's always treacherous to predict what people will find collectible in the future, but if the past is any guide, you might see strong interest in the following sets:

LEGO IDEAS: These sets are fan created and only produced in limited runs. Each proposed set must be supported by 10,000 fans before the company considers developing a full toy. The 8-inch tall Exo Suit, #21109, quickly sold out and the Ghost-

LEGO has yet to produce an officially-licensed set or minifigs featuring Marvel Comics' *Fantastic Four* characters, but that hasn't stopped Chinese companies from making knock-off figures. These are easily found online for just a few dollars.

Courtesy of Ruben Saldana

busters Ecto-1, #21108, became a fan favorite and now often trades for $60 against its $49.99 suggested retail price. Among the designs being considered for future release include LEGO Lightsabers for Darth Vader and Luke Skywalker, The Hubble Space Telescope, and the title robot from Disney/Pixar's *WALL•E*.

COMPANY EXCLUSIVES: LEGO sets given to employees are highly sought after by collectors. A rare 2012 set of founder Ole Kirk's house, #4000007, trades for $400+ and a 2011 LEGO Duck, based on Kirk's original wooden form, brings $200+ if sealed. The LEGO HUB Birds, set #4002014, was gifted to employees in 2015. The set's five birds represent the five countries where LEGO hub offices are located. The set is already trading for $200+.

DISNEY PRINCESSES: A set devoted to Disney's *Frozen* animated feature was the hot toy for Christmas 2014. Shoppers eagerly paid 50 percent over the original retail price of $40 to get a mint condition set after LEGO experienced a delivery deal during the holidays.

MINIFIGS: The hot minifigures of 2015? My money's on Series 13's quirky Hot Dog Man and the oddly appealing Unicorn Girl, both of which readily sold for $10 each in the first few weeks after their debut.

LEGO REPRODUCTIONS

Recently fans have begun to see an influx of reproduction and bootleg LEGO figures and full sets appearing online on major ecommerce sites such as eBay, Amazon.com, and

Alibaba.com. They are not identified as LEGO but rather "Lego compatible" or "custom" and often sold under the brand names JOYJOYTOWN, DECOOL, Dr. Luck, or Oxford. Sellers are often based in the Chinese provinces of Jiangsu, and among the districts of the city of Shenzhen, Guangdong, China.

The toy's style leaves little doubt the forms were based on several different licensed properties. It is possible to buy sets of eight minifigures, which cross different licensed properties (in one case, characters from Marvel Comics, DC Comics, and *Teenage Mutant Ninja Turtles* are offered in one bootleg bundle).

LEGO has yet to produce an officially licensed set or minifigs featuring Marvel Comics' *Fantastic Four* characters or its Silver Surfer character. Yet a quick search on eBay turns up at least five dozen listings of figures complete with stands. In some cases, even the box style and designs are being reproduced as well as the bricks. The knockoffs are cleverly produced and look like they would fit in any collection.

If buying online, be skeptical of sellers located outside your own country or eBay sellers who have joined the site recently. Research the company's complete line and future releases on BrickPicker.com, Brickset.com or BrickLink.com. Dedicated collectors avoid buying bulk lots of minifigs, but only time will tell if even discerning buyers will be able to distinguish the real from the fakes as quality improves.

The LEGO 2015 Series 13 Minifigure line has already inspired a cult following for the more odd and curious figures. The Hot Dog Man and Unicorn Girl figures quickly sold for three times their retail price within the first few weeks of their debut, **$10 each**. *Courtesy of eBay*

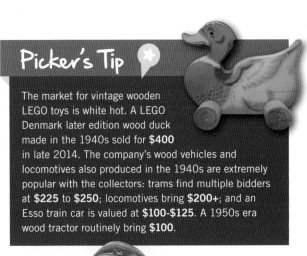

Picker's Tip ★

The market for vintage wooden LEGO toys is white hot. A LEGO Denmark later edition wood duck made in the 1940s sold for **$400** in late 2014. The company's wood vehicles and locomotives also produced in the 1940s are extremely popular with the collectors: trams find multiple bidders at **$225** to **$250**; locomotives bring **$200+**; and an Esso train car is valued at **$100-$125**. A 1950s era wood tractor routinely bring **$100**.

In 1932, carpenter Ole Kirk Kristiansen begins to manufacture wooden toys. The Duck is one of the most iconic wooden toys from the LEGO Group, which also included "pull-along" dogs, chickens, and even a monkey. So influential is this toy, in 2011 LEGO gave its employees a 91-piece brick version based on this original design, which itself now trades for **$150-$200**. It is estimated that only 100 of the ducks were made, according to Brickpedia.com.

Used by permission, ®2014 The LEGO Group

Made famous by the 1984 *Ghostbusters* film, the LEGO Ideas Ghostbusters ECTO-1 is the 006# user-designed product to be manufactured from the LEGO Ideas platform after receiving the requisite 10,000 fan votes to be considered for production, set #21108, **$100-$125**.

Used by permission, ®2014 The LEGO Group

LEGO Most Wanted

LEGO collectors are always on the hunt for complete, unopened sets from limited edition production runs. The following includes the most wanted sets and pieces; however, custom art creations - ranging from Zbigniew Liber's *LEGO-the concentration camp*, 1996, to Mario Minalie's *Red blue LEGO Chair*, 2007, for Droog design - have sold for $30,000-$10,000.

Millennium Falcon

The Millennium Falcon, set #10179, is the largest LEGO set ever made, with 5,195 pieces. At 33 inches long by 21 inches wide, the set was released in limited supply under the company's Ultimate Collector Series. The set is composed of 5,195 pieces and includes minifigs of fan favorites Chewbacca, Han Solo, Luke Skywalker, Princess Leia, and Obi-Wan Kenobi; **$2,000-$3,000 loose, $3,000-$4,500 sealed MIB.** *Courtesy of Eric Bradley*

LEGO Classic Town 6399

The Town Classic Airport Shuttle #6399 is a set of Town Airport released in 1990 with 767 pieces and 9 minifigures. It is one of the few electrified LEGO sets ever made, as a 9-volt battery powered the tram around the track; **$1,000-$4,000 sealed MIB.**

Another electrified set, the LEGO Technic Hauler #8264 has 574 pieces and a patented LEGO Power Functions tipping trailer bed. Even the steering system works on this toy, which also rebuilds into a flatbed trailer – twice the fun for one price; **$70-$150 sealed MIB**.

Death Star

The LEGO version of the *Star Wars* Death Star was an instant favorite by fans and collectors. There are two versions of this massive Ultimate Collector Series set: Death Star II, #10143, released in 2005, and Death Star #10188, released in 2008. Death Star II #10143 has 3,449 pieces and was retired in 2007 but was offered for sale until early 2009; **$2,600 sealed**. Death Star #10188 offers 24 minifigures, the most ever released with one set; **$350-$450 sealed MIB**.

Platinum Avohkii Mask of Light

The LEGO Bionicle line was launched in 2001 in an attempt to break into the world of action figures, animated television shows, online games, and comic books. The set issued Kanohi Masks worn by members of various warring races. The Platinum Avohkii Mask of Light was the grand prize in the Cartoon Network's Toonami Sweepstakes in October 2003. Chase Koches, then an 11-year old from Santa Clara, California, won the mask, which at the time was valued at $3,000. It is fashioned from three troy ounces of solid platinum, or about 93.31 grams. Koches sold the mask to Caleb Raff, owner of The Brick Hutt Lego store, who then sold it in February 2014 to collector Andre Hurley, 20, for $15,000, which is believed to be the highest price paid for a LEGO collectible. The auto glass repairman had already paid $3,000 for a gold Hau mask (one of five made) and the one-of-a-kind platinum mask was a crucial addition to his collection; **$15,000**.

Courtesy of Andre Hurley

"I Saw the Spectacular LEGO Village/ Jordan marsh" rare promotional button, pinback, c. 1958, for a display at Jordan Marsh Boston store (throughout the 1960s-1970s, Jordan Marsh's Enchanted Village was an annual display at its Downtown Crossing store to mark the holiday shopping season), mint, 2-1/4" w, **$51**.

In 2012, the LEGO Group launched LEGO Friends, a product line targeted at girls.

Set in Heartlake City, the LEGO® Friends play theme launched in 2012 is constructed around the five friends, Andrea, Emma, Mia, Olivia, and Stephanie, and their distinct personalities and interests and represents a new collectible toy line marketed to girls, set #41008, **$75-$100**.

Building kit, 1955, by Practi-Cole Products, Walt Disney's Alamo Construction Set, cylindrical plastic container with illustrated cardboard insert, features image of Fess Parker as Davy and back has instructions, 140 of red plastic LEGO-style bricks remain as well as container of adobe clay and additional instruction booklet, the clay was used to give the assembled fort a realistic look, scarce, excellent, **$229**.

This construction set recreates the iconic Simpsons family house in LEGO form. Included in the set is the entire family: Homer, Marge, Bart, Lisa, and Maggie, along with neighbor, Ned Flanders, set #71006, **$300-$350**. *Used by permission, ®2014 The LEGO Group*

The legendary Sopwith Camel, the aircraft flown by WWI aces and one of the most recognizable British aircraft to take to the skies, has been recreated as a LEGO® Exclusive model in 2012, set #3451, **$300-$325**.

Used by permission, ®2014 The LEGO Group

The Japanese spacecraft Hayabusa is the second LEGO® CUUSOO release, available in Japan and on shop.LEGO.com in 2012. Hayabusa ("falcon" in English) is an unmanned spacecraft built by the Japan Aerospace Exploration Agency (JAXA), designed to travel to a small near-Earth asteroid named Itokawa and return sample material to Earth, set #21101, **$139**.

Used by permission, ®2014 The LEGO Group

Created by real-life geoscientist, Ellen Kooijman (alias: Alatariel), the LEGO Ideas Research Institute is the 008# user-designed product to be manufactured from the LEGO Ideas platform after receiving the requisite 10,000 fan votes to be considered for production. The set depicts three varied professions within the world of natural science, comprising of a paleontologist studying the origin of dinosaurs with a magnifying glass, an astronomer with a telescope trying to map the sky, and a chemist carrying out experiments in a lab, set #21109, **$120-$150**.

Used by permission, ®2014 The LEGO Group

In 1978, the LEGO mini figures with movable arms and legs was introduced. Each generally consisting of nine to 10 parts, more than 4 billion mini figures had been made during the last 30 years. A set of these classic, vintage space astronauts from 1978 (white, red, yellow, blue, and black) with original oxygen tanks, sold for **$73**. A set of four with the original loose Cosmic Voyager, set #6985, trades for **$150+**.

Used by permission, ®2014 The LEGO Group

In May 2010, LEGO launched unique collectible figures in 16-figure series sets. Retailing for $2.99 to $3.99 each, the series is still growing strong and collectors have paid northwards of $2,000 for a set of 1,000. The most valuable single figures are those issued at exclusive events, such as New York's Toy Fair or the San Diego Comic-Con, which can sell for **$1,000-$2,000 a set.** *Courtesy of Eric Bradley*

NBA Collectors, set #3562, 11 pieces, **$25-$30**; NBA Collectors, set #3566, 10 pieces, **$20-$25**.

Courtesy of Eric Bradley

Figure, circa 2002, Jango Fett lifesize, The Lego Group, Denmark, one-of-a-kind retail display constructed of thousands of ordinary LEGO pieces; originally exhibited at San Diego Comic-Con, and then displayed at a now-defunct Toys R' Us, this is an incredibly detailed rendering of the *Star Wars* bounty hunter; each LEGO piece is permanently glued together and comes complete in the original cast-metal rolling display stand with custom Plexiglas sides that protect it while allowing for full viewing. Sure to be the definitive centerpiece of any *Star Wars* or LEGO collection, and among the first of these incredible LEGO sculptures ever offered for sale, mint, 36" w x 50" h. It was sold at public auction on Sept. 6, 2014 for **$5,100** and resold three days later on eBay for **$12,000**. *Courtesy of Morphy Auctions*

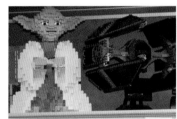

From LEGO Ultimate Collector's Series, set #7194 offered 1,078 pieces and is now valued at **$150 loose, $400-$500 sealed MIB**. On the right, the LEGO *Star Wars* TIE Interceptor, #6206, is valued at **$200** loose with its custom stand. *Courtesy of Eric Bradley*

LEGO *Star Wars* minifigures are sought after for both replacements to lost set pieces or as standalone collectibles. Values vary from **$5** to as much as **$750** for a rare, solid bronze LEGO *Star Wars* Boba Fett Minifigure, just two of which were given away by LEGO on May 4, 2011 to celebrate Star Wars Day (May The Fourth Be With You). *Courtesy of Eric Bradley*

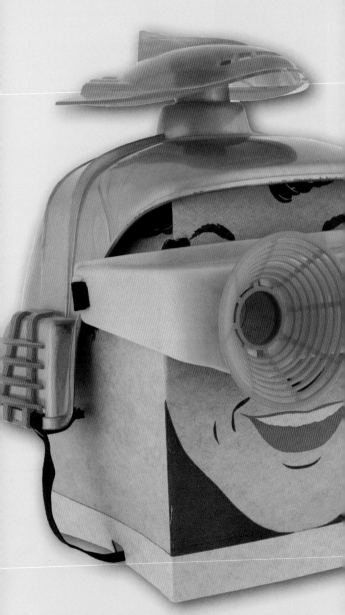

Space Helmet and glasses, circa early 1950s, Banner Plastics Corp, helmet and glasses come with original illustrated die-cut cardboard insert that is designed to look like a head which helmet and glasses rest on, excellent, **$546**. *Courtesy of Hakes Americana & Collectibles*

CHAPTER 9

Space Toys

In the Museum of Modern Art exhibition, *Century of the Child: Growing by Design 1900-2000*, an unusual star of the show was a space helmet with radar goggles from 1953. The odd design by Banner Plastics of Patterson, New Jersey, encompasses a lot of the big dreams and small toys produced in this era. From Hungary to Japan to New Jersey, rockets and space explorer toys were produced all over the world.

The Golden Age of space toys, as defined by variety and value, spans nearly 50 years (1925-1975). There are two primary drivers behind this boon: the 20th century space race and its pop-culture constructs.

The science fiction franchises ranging from *Buck Rogers* to *Lost in Space* to *Star Trek* made the space race real for children through its toys and radio shows.[21] Decades later, these toys now regularly bring five figures at auction. A bright red Machine Man tin robot – one of the Masudaya Gang of Five produced in Japan from the late 1950s through the early 1960s – sold at Sotheby's in December 1997 for $74,000. It still holds the record as the most valuable toy robot sold at public auction.

The sale was one of several high-profile auctions of tin robots in the late 1990s and early 2000s – including the storied collection of F.H. Griffith.[22] It coincided with a massive exhibit

---

21 I am not including *Star Wars* toys in this chapter simply because the toys and story belong to a modern era of space operas, rather than the wonder of space and its exploration.

22 Let the next two books you buy on this topic be *Blast Off!: Rockets, Robots, Ray Guns, and Rarities from the Golden Age of Space Toys*, and the Sotheby's auction catalog for the F.H. Griffith collection, December, 9, 2000.

of the Robert Lesser Collection of robots and space toys at the Museum of Science and Industry from late 2001 through 2002. This five-year period brought space toy collecting to the mainstream like never before ... and values have been flying as high as Sputnik ever since.

"Space toys have been popular since the 1930s, spurred on by the rise in popularity of the Buck Rogers and Flash Gordon comic strips, but after World War II, space toys enjoyed a huge increase in popularity, as the public became more intrigued with technology and the start of the Nuclear Age," said Greg Holman, lifelong fan of space toys. Holman knows his stuff: He is a cataloger at Heritage Auctions, a television personality, and is also known as the Pop Culture Guru of Facebook.

"In the 1970s, the release of George Lucas' *Star Wars* film series began what would become the largest space toy franchise in history. And while popularity of the *Star Wars* toys has only slightly diminished over the past decade, it appears that serious space toy collectors are gravitating towards vintage Japanese, British, and American rockets, ray guns, and robots, from the 1950s and 60s."

Original, unopened or un-played-with, mint in-box toys are garnering the highest prices at auction, with examples such as a Masudaya battery-operated Target Robot with original pictorial box and sealed bag of accessories selling for $52,900 and a mint pair of Marx Buck Rogers Rocket Skates in their original box selling for more than $8,500.

ADVERTISING SPACE TOYS

A popularly collected subset of space toy was produced as part of advertising campaigns, primarily from 1955 through 1970. Values drop drastically after this period simply because it seems people just stopped throwing things away – there is a surplus of items from this period.

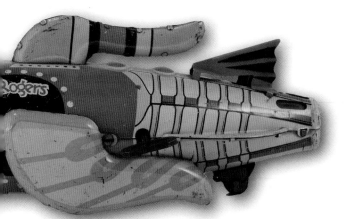

Marx Buck Rogers Rocket Ship wind-up toy, patent dated March 15, 1927, tin litho, 12-1/5" l, **$597**. *Courtesy of Heritage Auctions*

Scarce Buck Rogers in the 25th Century outfit, marked John Dille Co. 1934, by Sackman Bros. New York City, size 10, with rare original box, extremely difficult to find especially in box, excellent, 14-1/4" l, **$3,300**. *Courtesy of Morphy Auctions*

TANG, a staple in practically every American household from its 1957 debut through the 1980s, produced a number of space toys. The drink didn't hit peak popularity until kids everywhere heard John Glenn was drinking it in orbit in Friendship 7 (1962) and on later Gemini Program missions. A TANG inflatable Apollo Space Capsule ceiling display toy, dating from the late 1960s, is valued at $200 in today's market.

A famous form of toy mechanical bank was produced as a premium blank that could be customized by banks across the nation. The STRATO Rocket Bank and the Mercury Rocket Bank were made with a turquoise blue metal finish. A mint version with the original box can bring $120 to $150.

ALLURE OF SPACE

Marketers applied a space theme in some pretty odd and logic-defying ways during the 1950s and 1960s. Take the Japanese tin Volkswagen R-10 car with a spaceman behind the wheel and carton of atomic doohickeys in the backseat. The rare car brought $5,700 in late 2014. How this car was going to be useful in the vacuum of space wasn't part of the design plan and that's just why I think the toy is sought after by collectors. The inability of today's society to suspend disbelief puts these space-themed toys in a new, albeit campy, light. The tin Space Patrol Super Cycle Friction toy made by Bandai, features a rubber astronaut driver scooting along in a battery-powered fury of white sparks and a rotating antenna. What? The original box imaginatively shows a team of astronauts lifting off from the surface of a strange new world thanks to the powerful cycle. It's a beautiful, futuristic-looking space toy and also sold for $5,700.

Other odd space toys from this era include the tin litho friction Space Bus by Usagiya ($4,500), ROSKO's battery-operated Mobile Space T.V. Unit with trailer ($4,200). Perhaps nothing is more odd than Yoshia's downright kooky tin litho Space Elephant. The wind-up toy is about 5 inches long and has a weird coiled trunk and an atomic symbol printed on its chest. The strange toy sells for around $2,400 in excellent condition with the original box.

WHERE TO FIND THEM

If you're not the type to advertise or haunt estate sales, a good source for space toys is by online auction sites.

Space Elephant, circa
1950s, Yoshia, original
box, red tin litho, key
wind, 9" l, **$500-$600**.
Courtesy of ToyTent.com

eBay: The mega auction site uses listing categories to sort
Space Toys toys as follows: Toys & Hobbies » Robots, Monsters
& Space Toys » Space Toys » Pre-1970 » Tin » 1970-Now. The site
also breaks down toys for collectors and hobbyists or kids as
well as two main makers: Hasbro and Mattel. In early 2015, the
number of Robots (8,000+) listed were greater than the number
of Space Toys (4,000+) two-to-one. It's harder to get a deal, but
then again, deals do not a collection make. The site is a magnet
for novice sellers who post unique discoveries all the time. You
might pay more, but you'll also increase your chances of finding a really amazing toy.

ProxiBid: This site is an online auction source used by
many mid-tier auction and rural country auction houses. These
houses often do not have the ad budgets compared to specialty
houses, but they come across wonderful space toys all the time.
These are usually pulled directly from basements and attics
and are often found in "farm fresh" condition. A recent search
turned up several toys from estates in Minnesota, Nebraska,
Indiana and Pennsylvania. Rather than work with individual
sellers, on ProxiBid your bid is with an auction house with
established shipping methods. Pay special attention to any
extra fees charged as buyer's premiums. TIP: You can often
find a bargain if the auction is exclusively carried via ProxiBid
because fewer collectors are bidding on each lot. You will pay a
premium to bid through the site in addition to any fees charged
by the auction house.

LiveAuctioneers: Another online auction solution for auction houses, this site includes an increasing amount of lots by

overseas auctioneers – many of which are new to American bidders. At any given time there's a dozen or more space toys listed in upcoming auctions all over the world. The site also features a fully-illustrated free listing of previously-sold items. This is a good pricing service to help you gauge the values of similar toys sold at auction. I find it more valuable than eBay's completed and sold results because LiveAuctioneers' data reaches back 10 years or more. You will pay a premium to bid through the site in addition to any fees charged by the auction house.

SPACE ALWAYS HOT

Even contemporary toy makers are producing collector-quality space-themed toys. The 1995 Pixar Animation film, *Toy Story*, turns 20 years old in 2015 and original toys from the series are starting to see some interest among collectors. A 12-inch Utility Belt Buzz Lightyear (#64023) from Thinkway Toys' 2010 Toy Story Signature Collection line now trades for between $350 and $500, mint in box. Loose versions can sell for $100 to $200. The highly detailed film-inspired replica features a moving head and electronic phrases by actor Tim Allen's character from *Toy Story 2*.

Buzz Lightyear is likely the newest spaceman to hit the collecting scene, but a number of classic robots and other toys are favorite subjects for reproductions in today's market. It makes the supply of classic toys drives prices beyond the reach of the average collector then companies step in to make affordable toys. A series of Chinese-made tin wind-up robots have flooded the market in recent years. Priced at $6 and up, the 5-1/2-inch toys move with a wind-up key.

Billiken robots made in Japan in the late 1980s and 1990s are now hot collector's items. Made for a variety of licensed properties ranging from Predator to Batman, the robots are finely made and nifty-looking. A wind-up Billiken robot depicting H.R. Giger's famous Alien creature is valued at $150 to $200 and a Devilman tin wind-up robot representing a character from the Japanese live action television show (*Debiruman*, 1972-73) is valued at $150. Buyers have paid up to $350 for a Tetsujin 28-inch tin wind-up robot. Many of the robots were made only for the Japanese market and the generation that enjoyed them the first time around is well poised to spend big dollars to enjoy them again as vintage collectibles.

Twirly Whirly Rocket Ride, Japan, Alps, boxed example, lithographed tin, battery-operated space toy, well designed, great graphics on lid, very good, 9" h, **$401**.

Courtesy of Bertoia Auctions

Space toys, circa 1930s, group, Flash Gordon rocket ship, Flash with ray gun in an open cockpit; Tom Corbett rocket ship, both toys created rocket sound and a flint in the rear causes sparks to fly out of the rear, 12" l, **$592 set**. Courtesy of James D. Julia Auctioneers, Fairfield, Maine, www.jamesdjulia.com

Rocket toy, Japan, tin litho, battery operated, original box with nice colorful label, rocket marked 23 on both sides and Winner on back tail fin, excellent, 6-1/4" l. **$210**.

Courtesy of Morphy Auctions

Buck Rogers Wood Model Set, 1934, six different boxed balsa wood models issued by Buck Rogers Co. of Chicago, IL., ©1934 John F. Dille Co., sold in stores and offered as premiums, includes single original 3" x 7" x 2-1/2" d box with all ships in set: No. 1 Buck Rogers Battle Cruiser BC77Y, No. 2 Buck Rogers Martian Police Ship MP83Z, No. 3 Buck Rogers Flash Blast Attack Ship TS310Z, No. 4 Buck Rogers Super Dreadnought SD51X, No. 5 Buck Rogers Venus Fighting Destroyer FD69Z, No. 6 Buck Rogers Pursuit Ship PS91ZX. Completing this lot are seven professionally custom hand-crafted ships by Keith Kaonis, known for his one-of-a-kind wooden Disney and other folk art creations, **$4,362**.

All photos courtesy of Hakes Americana & Collectibles

Original box.

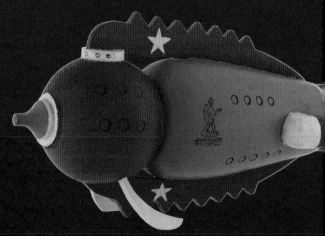

No. 2 Buck Rogers Martian Police Ship MP83Z.

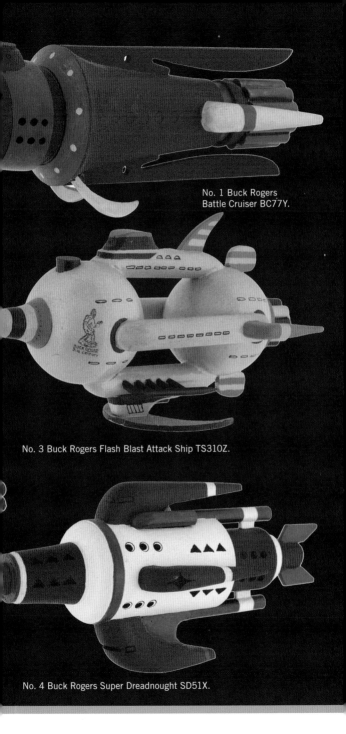

No. 1 Buck Rogers
Battle Cruiser BC77Y.

No. 3 Buck Rogers Flash Blast Attack Ship TS310Z.

No. 4 Buck Rogers Super Dreadnought SD51X.

ROBOTS

The market for vintage robots captures headlines every few months. Driven by more than 900 variations that exist and new discoveries, collectors have no shortage of robots to pursue. They are a uniquely Japanese development, born of the post-war economy, leftover factory tin and ingenuity. It was a booming cottage industry in Japan, one that more resembled the American tin toy industry of the mid-1840s. Small shops specialized to create parts which were passed to assembly plants and then to large distribution companies such as Maru-san and Yonezawa. The very earliest robots were produced of factory scrap, but that had ended by the 1950s. A stronger export market, a strong middle class consumer culture, and a global passion for all things relating to outer space sparked a new golden age for the tin robot.

A few of these mechanized marvels have gained mainstream status:

Gang of Five Robots

Now reproduced, the Masudaya Gang of Five were originally made by Modern Toys (Masudaya of Tokyo) at 15 inches each and included:

- **Radicon Robot:** the world's first wireless radio remote controlled robot, second ever radio controlled toy, 30-40 known to exist.
- **Giant Sonic Robot** - also known as Train robot, advances with swinging arms, flashing lights and a train whistle.
- **Non Stop Robot** - sometimes called Lavender robot or Lady robot due to its lavender color; advances, flashing lights, claws on arms that can grasp and hold objects.
- **Target Robot** - dart-shooting robot with toy gun and darts and target on his chest.
- **Machine Man Robot** - ordered

Robot, circa 1950s-early 1960s, Machine Man, Modern Toys, Japan, original, battery-operated, one of the gang of five, 14-3/4" h, **$44,850** (against $15,000 estimate). *Courtesy of Philip Weiss Auctions*

specially by a USA importer, therefore limited edition and never showed up in a catalogue like the other four, fewer than 10 to 15 known to exist, discovered again in 1997 as the miraculous fifth member of the Gang of Five, according to Picollecta.com, Wikicollecting Blog.

A Target Robot smashed a world auction record for an example of its type when it ended at $52,900 in 2010, triple the previous auction record set in 2008. The toy robot still not only retained its rare original box but also its shooting accessories were offer still intact in the original sealed bag.

The record for a Target Robot still doesn't come close to the $74,000 paid for a Machine Man Robot sold at a December 1997 Sotheby's auction – still the record for the most valuable robot ever sold at public auction. Other examples come up for sale since and have sold for five figures as well. Given the variety, history and direction our post-modernist society, the toy robot is likely to remain a popular collectible for generations.

Robots, circa 1968-77, Ideal Toys, complete set of six Zeroid Robots and original box, from Zeroid Commander Action Set, figures: 5" h to 7"h, **$350**. *Courtesy of Thomaston Place Auctions*

Robot, 1975, Palitoy Ltd., Doctor Who "Talking Dalek," © BBC, based on the robotic/mutant nemesis of the long-running British sci-fi hero Dr. Who, produces phrases, "What Are Your Orders?," "Exterminate!," "Attack! Attack! Attack!," "You Will Obey!" fine, toy: 6-1/4", **$151**.

Courtesy of Hake's Americana & Collectibles

Robot, Inter Planet Space Captain, Aoshin Shoten, Japan, tin litho, wind-up, original box, excellent, scarce and desirable robot, 8" h, **$19,800**. *Courtesy of Morphy Auctions*

Target Robot, Masuadaya, from original Gang O Five set, battery-operated, unused condition with cardboard insert and headpiece, original gun and darts still sealed in bag, scarce, original box, near mint, 15" h, **$52,900**. *Courtesy of Morphy Auctions*

Wind-up Television Robot, Japan, made by Kanto, working, original box, excellent-near mint, 8" h, **$32,400**. *Courtesy of Morphy Auctions*

Robot, 1990s, Billiken, Tetsujin tin litho, wind-up, original box, marked "28" on box and toy and "Osaka Tin Toy institute," near mint, box: 9-1/2" h, **$210**.
Courtesy of Morphy Auctions

Robot, 1990s, Billiken, Tetsujin, tin litho, wind-up, original box, marked "28" on box and toy and "Osaka Tin Toy institute," near mint, box: 9-1/2" h, **$300**.
Courtesy of Morphy Auctions

RAY GUNS

A throwback to a different time, the space ray gun was an important tool in every spaceman and gal's mission to defend the cosmos from alien threats. The most valuable space gun sold in recent years is a store display set of PEZ candy shooters, which hammered for $3,162. A follow up, selling for $2,280, is a circa 1960 battery-operated Electro Ray-Gun made by Yonezawa in its original box.

Toy gun, circa 1950s, PEZ, original store display board with six hard plastic original space-themed candy dispensers each 5" l, text: "49¢ Loaded/Price Includes Genuine PEZ Space Gun Permit," display: 9-1/2" w x 13-1/2"h, **$3,162**. *Courtesy of Hakes Americana and Collectibles*

Toy gun, circa 1960, Japanese Tin Litho Electro Ray-Gun, Yonezawa, tin litho, plastic front, battery operated, original box, excellent, 10" l, **$2,280** (against $100 estimate). *Courtesy of Morphy Auctions*

Toy gun, 1946, Buck Rogers Atomic Pistol U-238, Daisy, considered the last of the classic Buck Rogers metal toy zap-guns, produced with a gold finish and sold in stores, fine, **$358**. *Courtesy of Heritage Auctions*

Marx Tin Litho Tom Corbett Space Pistol, includes scarce original box, marked "Rockhill Productions," very good–excellent, 10" l, **$780**. *Courtesy of Morphy Auctions*

Buck Rogers Disintegrator Pistol, Daisy, unusual copper coloring, marked "Buck Rogers 25th Century," box marked "Model XZ-38," scarce, box (very good), gun (excellent), 9-1/2" l, **$1,920**.

Courtesy of Morphy Auctions

Toy water gun, Hiller Atomic Ray Gun, spring pump mechanism, scarce original box, 7" l, **$3,000** (against a $400 estimate).

Courtesy of Morphy Auctions

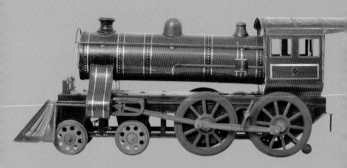

Gunthermann, Germany, tin litho wind-up locomotive, retains ringing bell underneath, C8, **$450**. *Courtesy of Stout Auctions, stoutauctions.com*

Lionel, prewar O gauge 2226W tender, **$2,400**. *Courtesy of Stout Auctions, stoutauctions.com*

Locomotive, Schoenner, Germany, Gauge 5, early, boxed set, mostly nickeled overall, red painted spoke wheels, together with tin coach with steps and bench seating, 7" l, **$2,778**. *Courtesy of Stout Auctions, stoutauctions.com*

CHAPTER 10

Model Trains

The model train market is reliably immune to wild swings in prices. The collector and seller in this genre enjoys all the benefit of steady demand without any of the fluctuations in prices seen in other hobbies, such as vintage advertising signs.

Collectors are a devoted and fraternal group and probably the most social in all toy collecting. That can partially be attributed to the fact that the trains are the "gateway collectible" into a much deeper and engrossing hobby of modeling projects. Track plans are endless and unlike any other toy genre, a busy industry is still creating new and innovative structures.

Collectors often specialize by make and model. The earliest toys were floor trains, which date to the 1840s. Wood was the first material used for these toys with pressed steel, tin, and cast iron used in the early 1860s. Victorian model railway toys saw the rise of steam engines that operated without the need for a track. These simple steam toys are often called "dribblers," "piddlers," or some variation thereof because the engines often left a small trail of water behind them. These toys were reproduced between 1970 through the 1990s in brass kits that are still seen on the market or in estate sales.

Retailers began to develop rail-system train sets beginning in the 1880s, steam and wind-up (clockwork) powered of course. For the next 20 years, the number of train makers grew exponentially to include Marklin, Bing, Carette & Cie, and Issmayer (all from Germany) led the market with innovations which are pursued by collectors 120 years later. In particular, Carette trains are known for realistic and complex designs with high-quality clockwork mechanism. A Carette Gauge I No. 2350 locomotive and tender, considered the finest American steam profile locomotive ever produced, sold at auction in 2011 for $30,250.

The turn of the 20th century saw the standardization of

model train gauges. You can thank the British toy maker Bassett-Lowke for the development as they worked to create toys true to scale of real working trains. This standardization means collectors can connect trains made decades apart and by different companies if the cars are of the same gauge. Simply, the gauge is width of the track. Although the terms are sometimes used interchangeably, technically *gauge* is different than *scale* in that scale refers to the size relationship between a model and its real-world example. Based on these scales and gauges, the most commonly collected American train makers are Lionel, American Flyer, Marx, and Ives.

Lionel was the leading 20th century toy train manufacturer: By 1930 it owned Ives, during the 1950s it was selling $25 million in trains per year, and by 1968 it owned American Flyer. A bankruptcy four months later spelled the end of the company and an end of an era. Train collectors consider 1969 the last year of "authentic" Lionel trains, although the 1970s ushered in a new dawn in plastic toys.

Lionel created some of the most desirable toy train sets that are still hotly sought after today, although collectors remain picky about condition. A few highlights:

Mickey Mouse Circus Train: No. 1536 features a windup O gauge train set complete with a "Mickey Mouse Circus" car (#1536), a "Circus Dining Car" (#1518), and "Mickey Mouse Band" car (#1536), a paper circus tent, a large Mickey Mouse barker composite figure, and assorted cardboard cutout pieces. A set in top condition sold for $9,858 in early 2014.

Santa Fe Twin Engine: Introduced in 1948 was the company's top train with variations selling well for years. An Aluminum Super Speedliner Passenger Set 2190W, circa 1953, containing 2353P/2353T Santa Fe F3 AA diesel units, 2354 Silver Bluff Pullman, 2353 Silver Cloud Pullman, 2532 Silver Range Vista Dome, 2351 Silver Dawn observation cars sold for $2,900 at auction in early 2015.

Lionel, rare postwar gray 3562-1
red letter barrel car, C6+, **$2,700.**

Courtesy of Stout Auctions, stoutauctions.com

1930s Lionel engines and tender: These remain a collector favorite and the early 1930s 260E Stream Engine and the 400E steamer is considered the pinnacle of Lionel's designs. A No. 241E O Gauge Passenger Set along with a No. 260E engine and two No. 710 blue passenger cars sold for $5,300 at auction in 2006.

Post-war sets: Sets such as a Lionel Congressional Passenger Set No. 2254W are in demand. A mint matched original set from 1955 brought $11,000 in January 2015 at Stout Auctions, the leading auctioneer of vintage scale and toy trains.

Model trains' leading challenge is attracting enough new fans who can afford to spend the time and money it takes to build wonderful sets. In America, the golden age of American railroading ended in the late 1970s, which is roughly the tail end of Generation X. This is the first American generation that did not grow up with trains as a force in either popular culture or in commerce and that worries some train collecting veterans. Nevertheless, collectors are still joining this hobby and bringing curiosity and ingenuity along for the ride.

Get Info: Kalmbach Publishing produces five railroading-related magazines including *Model Railroader, Trains, Classic Toy Trains*, and *Garden Railways*. *Classic Trains* focuses on the golden years of American railroading from the 1920s to the late 1970s. Learn more at trc.trains.com.

Lionel sold 253,000 of this Mickey Mouse hand car (1100) in 1934. This rare variant with a green body is much harder to find than the common red body, C7, **$525**. *Courtesy of Stout Auctions, stoutauctions.com*

Pre-War Mickey Mouse Circus Train Set #1536 (Lionel, 1935), a holy grail of Mickey Mouse (and Lionel Trains) collectibles. The original box includes the locomotive (#1508), a stoker tender car (with a shoveling Mickey), a "Mickey Mouse Circus" car (#1536), a "Circus Dining Car" (#1518), and "Mickey Mouse Band" car (#1536), the tracks (two straight sections and six curved), a paper circus tent, a large Mickey Mouse barker composite figure, and assorted cardboard cutout pieces. The box is 11-1/4" x 17" x 2-1/4" and the composite Mickey figure is 5" h and made from compressed sawdust. The only items that seem to be missing are three of the 5-cent tickets (one has been folded and tucked inside one of the cars) and the locomotive windup key. This is one of the most complete sets in existence of one of the most desirable toys from the 1930s, and is highly sought after and coveted by Disney, toy, and train collectors alike, **$9,858**.
Courtesy of Heritage Auctions

Lionel, 1906-07 prewar No. 2 Electric Rapid Transit Trolley, C7, **$5,586.** *Courtesy of Stout Auctions, stoutauctions.com*

TRAINS GRADING GUIDE

The following condition and grading standards are used by the Train Collectors Association and have been adopted by respected train auction houses and collectors. These standards apply to all toy train and related accessory items, not just locomotives and cars. Whether a toy train operates does not change or influence these standards; boxes do not fall under these guidelines and are always evaluated separately. *Source: Traincollectors.org*

C1 ....Junk-parts value only

C2 ....Restoration required

C3 ....Poor; requires major body repair: heavily scratched, major rust, missing parts, major restoration candidate

C4 ....Fair, scratched: moderate, paint loss, dented, missing parts, surface rust, evidence of heavy use

C5 ....Good; signs of play wear: with scratches and minor paint loss, small dents, minor surface rust, evidence of heavy use

C6 ....Very good: minor scratches and paint nicks, minor spots of surface rust, free of dents, may have minor parts replaced

C7 ....Excellent-all original: minute scratches and paint nicks, no rust, no missing parts, no distortion of component parts

C8 ....Like New-complete all original: No rust, no missing parts, may show affects of being on display and/or age, may have been run

C9 ....Factory New-brand new: all original, unused, may evidence factory rubs and the slightest evidence of handling, shipping and having been test run at the factory

C10 ..Mint-brand new: all original, unused and unblemished

Train collecting is handed down from generation to generation and toy shows are an ideal source for sets, cars, and information on what's selling.
Courtesy of Jack Kelly

Lionel, postwar O gauge 1587S Girls train in brick original boxes with original set box, with a 2037-500 loco, 1130T-500 tender, 6462-500 New York Central canister car, 6464-515 M-K-T boxcar, 6464-510 New York Central boxcar, 6436-500 Lehigh Valley hopper car and a 6427-500 Pennsylvania caboose, and the 1043-500 transformer, C9+, **$4,900**. *Courtesy of Stout Auctions, stoutauctions.com*

Lionel prewar standard gauge brown state set with a 408E center cab electric locomotive, 412 California, 413 Colorado, 414 Illinois and 416 New York passenger and observation cars, all original, C6, **$16,500** after 223 bids. *Courtesy of Stout Auctions, stoutauctions.com*

Voltamp, 2100 Baltimore and Ohio steam locomotive and tender with original paint, engine: 15" l, tender: 9-1/4" l, C7, **$7,500**.

Courtesy of Stout Auctions, stoutauctions.com

Lionel, modern G Scale Thomas and Friends set in OB, Set 81011, factory sealed, C10, **$120**. *Courtesy of Stout Auctions, stoutauctions.com*

Lionel, prewar green 3659 dump car, rare color variant to standard red, C7+, **$1,600**. *Courtesy of Stout Auctions, stoutauctions.com*

This true rarity and museum-quality Pinard three-wheel motorcycle in the Donald Kaufman collection quickly caught the eyes of collectors when it went up for auction. Created in France in 1905, the two-cylinder-style cycle is 14" l and highly detailed with opening doors and a realistic looking motor. The driver itself is articulated and moves in his seat. It sold for **$23,000**.

Courtesy Bertoia Auctions

This Arcade Red Baby International Harvester truck is the first toy ever purchased by Don Kaufman, whose family founded KB Toys. Don's world renowned collection eventually sold for more than $12 million. This toy was presented to his widow, Sally Kaufman, from Bertoia's Auction and members of the toy collecting community.

Courtesy Bertoia Auctions

Tin rocket toy, Kokyu, circa 1950s, Jet Rocket V-7, Japanese space rocket, friction drive sparking mechanism, scarce, 19" l, from the Yoku Tanaka Toy Collection, **$5,000**.

Courtesy of Bonhams

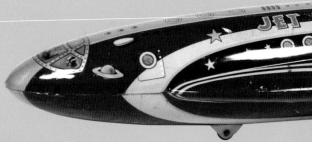

CHAPTER 11

Toy Vehicles

Miniature versions of full-size cars, tanks, planes, and boats have been around as long as the originals, of course, but today's market is dominated by Hot Wheels, Matchbox, and vintage tin.

The "Daimler" clockwork horseless carriage tin toy, made by Bing in 1901, is one of the first tin cars based on designs of Gottlieb Daimler's first motor vehicle. The 7-1/2-inch toy with two figures features a clockwork mechanism under a riding passenger and sold for roughly $2,500 in 2011. In the 114 years since, the variety of vehicle toys is only limited to imagination. To date, there has only been one collection that touched every corner of the toy vehicle market and Donald Kaufman wanted to share it with the world. Assembled over a 60-year period, Kaufman's passion spanned American, Japanese, and European autos, boats, trucks, and farm toys. He literally did not know how many toys he owned when the collection was packed up for auction. The final count reached some 7,000 and realized more than $12 million over three years.

Kaufman's family founded K·B Toys. His series of auctions spanning 2009 through 2011 was billed as a once-in-a-lifetime buying opportunity and in many cases, bidders far exceeded pre-auction estimates. Come to find out, even high

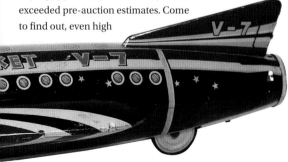

Car, Hot Wheels, 1970, Hong Kong Custom Firebird, retaining its original button and back card in French and printed in Germany, **$2,999**.

Courtesy of eBay

bids were bargain buys. In the years since the last auction, prices for items from the auction have been climbing. A single fig- ural metal and glass candy container in the form of a gas pump sold as a set for $162.50 in the fourth Kaufman auction in 2010, but it resurfaced on eBay in early 2015 for $275.[23]

An unopened box of 96 Hot Wheels dated to 1970 reached a high bid of **$40,200** on eBay following 109 bids in early 2014. The box failed to reach the seller's mandated reserve. *Courtesy of eBay*

Perhaps what set Kaufman's collection apart from any other was its outstanding condition and near fanatical level of completeness. No two toys were alike and each represented the absolute finest example known to exist. True rarities in the collection quickly caught the eyes of collectors, especially a rare and museum-quality Pinard three-wheel motorcycle. Created in France in 1905, the two-cylinder-style cycle is 14 inches long and highly detailed with opening doors and a realistic looking motor. The driver itself is articulated and moves in his seat. Esti-

23 Lot 4589, a lot of two gas candy containers for $325, Sept. 25, 2010.

Parts for Hot Wheels Redlines are sometimes easier to find than parts for the authentic cars. Brian Listman of Christmas 1970 Restorations provides custom repairs to original vintage toy cars. Prices and styles span the most desirable models from 1968-1977 and are priced from **$30 to $45 each**.

Courtesy of Eric Bradley

mated to sell for at least $10,000, the motorcycle sold for $23,000.

Condition influences vehicle values tremendously, mostly because these types of toys were intended to be played

Picker's Tip

The date on a Hot Wheels is not the year when it was made. It is the year of the design copyright.

with – and 98 percent of them were. This is especially the case with Hot Wheels toys, says Brian Listman, a Hot Wheels dealer and owner of Christmas 1970 Restoration. Naming his business after the most memorable holiday of his childhood, Listman's eBay store specializes in preservation materials to keep the 1:64 diecast cars free from scratches. The plastic car cases are popular with collectors who find lose cars, he said, but he also sells special blister pack cases designed to protect the entire card and blister of any standard size 4-1/2-inch to 6-1/2-inch blistered card.

"Most all collectors are after the Hot Wheels Redlines," Listman said, referring to the line of diecast cars produced from 1968 to 1977 and so named for the red stripe on the tire sidewalls. With supply scarce, Listman has found a niche in restoring and refurbishing select cars and customizing certain models.

"The true value is in the muscle cars," he said. "The more they look like the original muscle cars made around that period the more popular they are."

Rare examples easily generate four-figure bids:

- In 2011, a Redline '73 Yellow Snake 2 from the collection of Hot Wheels mega-collector Mike Strauss sold for $5,100.
- A collection of 123 Redlines from the late 1960s and early 1970s sold for $3,726 on eBay in late 2014 following 24 bids.
- A rare, green chrome Hong Kong Custom Firebird, retaining its original button and back card in French and printed in Germany, sold for $2,999.
- In 2012, a Hot Wheels store display from 1970, decked out with 12 original Redlines in front of a sporty cardboard diorama backdrop sold for $3,690.
- A 1977 Datsun Z prototype, described as "possibly the only one in existence," was offered for $3,436 (that's after the 20 percent price drop from the seller's original $4,295 asking price). The prototype or "blank base" as they are described in the Hot Wheels world is claimed to be from the collection of a former Mattel employee.

These prices paid for day-to-day auctions pale in comparison for the five figure values that have come to dominate the top of the market. An unopened box of 96 Hot Wheels dated to 1970 reached a high bid of $40,200 on eBay following 109 bids in early 2014. The box failed to reach the seller's mandated reserve. Given that an original vintage Redline sells for between $1,000 and $2,000 online, that would mean the box's true worth would be near six figures.

That price pales in comparison to the most valuable Hot Wheels of all time: a 1969 Pink Rear-Loading Volkswagen Beach Bomb prototype - too wide to fit with the Hot Wheels Super Charger Spring set - valued at $72,000.

Pickers say the best places to locate vintage Hot Wheels are not where you'd expect. With the sweet spot of Hot Wheels Redlines just 47 to 38 years ago, many thousands are likely still sitting in the bottom of toy boxes all across the country. The key in finding vintage Hot Wheels on the cheap is to source them as close to the original owner as possible:

GARAGE SALES: The No. 1 source of vintage Hot Wheels.

Hot Wheels collectors easily defy logic when it comes to accumulating both quantity and quality. A Hot Wheels collector has literally covered the entrance to his basement with thousands of carded Hot Wheels cars.

Courtesy of Eric Bradley

YouTube is full of fun videos showing off garage sale scores of vintage Redlines. It's not surprising to see why. With a generational shift taking place across the United States, Baby Boomers are not cleaning out and downsizing the homes where they raised families. That means a lot of unwitting grandmas and grandpas are selling lots of vintage Hot Wheels. Show up to these sales early but if you come across a few rare finds then do your karma a favor and offer the seller more than what they're asking. There's a subtle way to do this without making a scene or dooming the sale.

FLEA MARKETS: Many pickers buy collections and sell them at fleas and swap meets. Great deals can be found at non-toy meets, especially monthly markets. Check out car swap meets, too, but keep your expectations for low prices in check. Lots of gear heads collect Hot Wheels so prices may be a bit high. They should still be lower than the final prices paid on mega sites like eBay.

COMMUNITY THRIFT STORES: These sites can be a gold mine of vintage Hot Wheels. The same rule of offering a fair price at garage sales applies at community thrift stores. This might matter more here since many community thrift stores support worthwhile charities in their communities.

OTHER COLLECTORS: Eliminate the middle man markup and deal with collectors. Many collectors are looking to fill holes in their collection. Several states have regional Hot Wheels clubs that meet to share information, organize shopping trips and hold members-only swap meets or silent auctions. Check out Mattel's club locator page off HotWheelsCollectors.com.

Tin car, Asahi, circa 1950s, a very good example of one of the most sought after Japanese toys of mid-century, original box, from the Yoku Tanaka Toy Collection, scarce, 15" l, **$17,500**. *Courtesy of Bonhams*

Early tin litho service station toy and early toy auto, England, excellent, 1-3/4" h x 2" d x 2-7/8" w, **$288**.

Courtesy of William Morford Investment Grade Collectibles at Auction

Tin car, Asakusa, circa 1950s, Japanese comic/adventure series tin vehicle, depicting three vinyl characters within lithographed American car, scarce, 15" l, from the Yoku Tanaka Toy Collection, **$3,500**.

Courtesy of Bonhams

Tin car, Nomura, circa 1960s, Volkswagen R-10 Beetle Concept Car, two-door tin convertible bump and go mechanism with astronaut, antenna and light panel, 12-1/5" l, from the Yoku Tanaka Toy Collection, **$4,750.**

Courtesy of Bonhams

Tin cars, Schuco, circa 1930s, lot including: Kommando Anno 2000 in green, no box; Examico 4001 in yellow, no box, US Zone; Tacho-Examico 4002 in wine, US Zone, in box with instructions; Bestuurbare Auto 3000 in flame red, with box, instructions, all accessories, two extra 'Fernlenks', **$767.** *Courtesy of Thomaston Place Auctions*

Cast iron vehicles, Arcade, circa 1960s, assortment of four (of the original five) small Arcade cast iron vehicles including a fire truck, wrecker, car and racing car, white rubber tires, (missing one car from the set) 4" to 5-1/5" l, **$478.**

Courtesy of Heritage Auctions

Tin car, Mitsuhashi, circa 1950s, Pontiac "Concept" Car, friction car with dual wind screens and tailfin; playwear to chrome and underside, from the Yoku Tanaka Toy Collection, scarce, 10" l, **$6,000**.

Courtesy of Bonhams

Motorcycle, Arnold, 1947, MAC 700, tin litho, Germany, Arnold maker's mark on front fender, 7-1/5" l x 4-1/2" h, **$418**.

Courtesy of Heritage Auctions

Truck, Marklin, circa 1930s, Standard Oil Tanker, a German clockwork, articulated wheels; excellent, 16" l, **$1,187**.

Courtesy of Bonhams

Truck, Keystone, circa 1920s, cast iron, embossed 3 Ton on sides of stake body, painted in orange overall, cast headlamps, red spoke wheels, red painted Keystone emblem on side, pressed steel flooring, very good, scarce, 12-1/4" l, **$1,605**. *Courtesy of Bertoia Auctions*

Tin car, Jep, circa 1920s, of the Jep series of automotive vehicles, enameled in dark blue with a nickel plated radiator and headlamps on either side, interior lever engages the mechanism in forward or reverse, steering is accomplished via the steering wheel within the vehicle, original box with directions, scarce, 13" l, **$3,555**. *Courtesy of James D. Julia Auctioneers, Fairfield, Maine, www. jamesdjulia.com*

Tractor, Dinky Toys No. 22e, in cream and red, **$100-$150**.

Courtesy of Toovey's Antique & Fine Art Auctioneers & Valuers

Bulldozer, Marx, circa 1940s, tin litho toy with pliable rubber tractor treads, wind-up action and lever controls driving when wound, working with key, original box, from the Don Maris Collection, 10-1/4" l x 6-7/8" h, **$345**.

Courtesy of Hakes Americana & Collectibles

Trencher, Buddy L, 1928, one of Buddy L's heaviest construction toys, large conveyor chute with trenching buckets, frame on traction treads, well scaled and detailed, good, rare, 20" w x 22" l, **$2,278**.

Courtesy of Bertoia Auctions

URANIUM RUSH

An exciting new electric game for the family

Make a million dollars!

YOUR 'GEIGER COUNTER' LIGHTS AND BUZZES YOUR WAY TO FUN AND FORTUNE

Toy game, 1950s, Uranium Rush, by Gardner Games, battery operated and of same design as electric quiz games of the time period, box reads, "Your Geiger Counter Lights And Buzzes Your Way To Fun And Fortune," while the large instruction sheet reads, "The Prospector With The Most Money In His Possession When All Claims Have Been Staked Wins The Game," battery-operated Geiger counter is a 5-1/2" h cardboard tube, complete with a light bulb mechanism, Geiger counter has an attached wire with metal tip that is to be placed on one of the many diecut mines and if uranium is found, a light bulb lights. Excellent, 14" x 21-1/2" x 1-1/5" d, **$60**.

Courtesy of Hakes Americana & Collectibles

CHAPTER 12

Oddities and Rarities

Excellent examples of key toys are the cornerstone of a great collection, but sometimes the toys that defy classification are the true standouts. Just like in music, the toy world is full of "one-hit-wonders" that take on a collectible appeal simply because of their strange and unusual nature. Perhaps they are prototypes that were never made, maybe they reflect a side of culture we'd all rather forget, perhaps they are nothing more than market failures. Whatever the reason, odd and unusual toys often take top lot honors and earn a proud place in many fine collections.

In almost all circumstances, the more unusual and ill-conceived a toy is, the more desirable it is. For instance, unproduced action figure prototypes are eagerly sought after because they represent an important part of a toy line's history. The Star Wars Collectors Archive shows nearly 650 action figure prototypes and conceptual figures spanning the sci-fi fantasy films, specials, and animated series.

Prototypes are especially popular among train collectors. With so many variations in production at one time, the occasional Lionel prototype can come to auction for thousands of dollars. A factory prototype of the #6427 Illuminated Lionel Lines N5C Caboose that Lionel modified in the 1950s featured an operating watchman that pops-out when the train is started. It lived in the private collection of a former Lionel employee for nearly 50 years before it sold for $2,450 at auction.

These toys usually "sell themselves" because they appeal to so many different types of collectors for so many different reasons. Although much more difficult to come by, oddities and unusual toys are often the cornerstones of coveted collections.

KIDDIE RIDES

Not every kid owned one, but every kid rode one. Coin-operated amusement rides for small children have been in use for the last 40 years. They are still found today, but vintage versions are highly collectible. Base rides are the most common but hydraulic, carousel, teeter totter, and bumper car-like rides are also collected. If you think the trend in owning one of these commercial rides is a niche, Denver's Kiddie Rides USA might disagree. The company has a booming business selling rides for use in private homes by collectors. New rides retail for about $5,000.

Among the most valuable vintage kiddie rides sold in the last few years include a circa 1950s base ride in the form of a 1950s racer for $3,500, a circa 1950s "Ride Tusko" elephant safari ride for $2,040, and a three-ride carousel ride with horses and a big-top tent motif for $500.

A circa-1953 fiberglass horse "Trigger" 10-cent machine was once exhibited at the Midwest Museum of American Art. Fully operational and professionally restored, the rider has large decals on each side reading, "Roy Rogers Double R Bar Ranch." It sold at an auction in Long Island for **$2,300**. *Courtesy of Philip Weiss Auctions*

This fantasy (not vintage) coin-op Indian motorcycle ride measures 53" h x 28" w x 54" l and sold for **$7,500** at auction. *Courtesy of Heritage Auctions*

Batmobile giant coin-operated ride, circa 1960s, 44" h, car measures approximately 65" l and 23-1/2" h, **$2,270**. *Courtesy of Heritage Auctions*

Action figure prototype, 1979, Alien figure for MAXx FX toy line, never-released, based on H.R. Giger's designs for the 1979 film, *Alien*, snap-on appliances, with shipping box with "Max Miracle Models" label, from the Mel Birnkrant Collection, 11" h, **$4,554**.
Courtesy of Hakes Americana & Collectibles

Puppets, set of three, circa 1940s, Three Stooges characters, heads made of painted composition material, with a felt body and hands, excellent, 11" h and 8" w, **$4,481**. *Courtesy of Heritage Auctions*

One of the ways in which the suffrage movement was promoted both here and in England was through the distribution of suffrage toys and spinners or whirl-a-gigs. There are three to four different examples of the latter, including this circa 1920 Whirl-a-Gig, maker unknown. One ring in white contains the message, "Votes for Women." The other ring, in yellow, suggests perhaps that this item may have been associated, in one fashion or another, with the Woman's Suffrage Party of New York. Tin, excellent, from the Frank Corbeil Collection, **$1,434**.
Courtesy of Heritage Auctions

Cap gun, 1890s, made in Connecticut, fancy figural animated "Shoot the Hat" (pulling trigger makes standing man leap forward to place hat on seated man- exploding the cap), Japanned surface, figure still has original wire beard, fine, 4-3/4" x 4-3/4" x 5/8", **$575**.

Courtesy of William Morford Investment Grade Collectibles at Auction

Toy, Mechanical Target, unusual, early tin wind-up mechanical target toy featuring moving gangster target heads at top of get-away car, excellent, 4-3/4" x 6-7/8" x 3-1/4", **$374**.

Courtesy of William Morford Investment Grade Collectibles at Auction

Toy cannon, circa 1914, by Marklin, large scale all metal model of WWI German Siege Howitzer "Big Bertha," blank firing, with bronze tube, bronze and brass recoil, steel breech, painted steel carriage with tractor pad wheels, Marklin tag on front, scarce, 8" barrel, 8" w, 18-1/2" l, **$4,400**.

Courtesy of Thomaston Place Auctions

Neil Armstrong, the first man to walk on the moon, was first a pilot. Perhaps he was inspired by this small toy airplane that was discovered in the attic of his childhood home in Wapakoneta, Ohio. Armstrong's family moved to the house in 1944 and stayed there until 1964. The new owners found this very cool red metal toy airplane, 9-1/2" l x 7" w, **$10,755**.

Courtesy of Heritage Auctions

TEARING IT UP: PAPER TOYS

Few paper toys were expected to survive rough and tumble childhood play. Those that did survive now command big prices among collectors. These ephemeral toys have tremendous cross-over appeal depending on the subject matter and even the function. Some mechanical paper toys far surpass their original intent and take on an engineering quality, whereas promotional toys appeal to advertising or premium collectors. It's easy to see why items such as paper dolls (aka dressing dolls) were so popular: easily

American Rangers Automatic Smoking Gun, circa 1930s, wood and cardboard gun comes with six paper packets of "Smoke Powder For American Rangers Automatic Absolutely Harmless," (chalk powder), when revolving trigger is fired, cardboard lever snaps and creates smoke effect, very good, 4" x 5-1/2" x 1/2", **$85**.

Courtesy of Hakes Americana & Collectibles

mass produced, the affordable toys could be constantly altered and changed with new clothes or accessories. The children themselves could draw and cut out their own custom creations as well. Shadow puppets were first produced of leather in Asia hundreds of years ago and the practice was adapted in Europe by 1800. English and German-made lithographed theaters are highly sought after: a paper and board theater from the collection of author and doll house museum founder Flora Gill Jacobs sold for $900 in early 2014.

Paper construction sets of circuses and theaters appeared in America in the 1870s and by the early 20th century, punch-out construction sets allowed kids to create space ships, homes, and action scenes.

Paper theater, circa 1900, maker unknown, the paper-covered wood base houses three sets of scenery panels, paper actors, as well as an elaborate and colorful three-part proscenium with fabric curtain; an unusual feature is the painted composition prompter's shell, 23" x 27", **$900.** *Courtesy of Noel Barrett Vintage Toys @ Auction, LiveAuctioneers*

Dancing Charlie Chaplin cardboard puppet, circa 1920s, British, cardboard figure of Charlie Chaplin with hinged legs, figure is excellent, original envelope is very good, 13-1/2" h, **$50-$75**.

Courtesy of Heritage Auctions

Submarine toy and clock, circa 1968-69, The Beatles Yellow Submarine, die-cast/plastic Corgi Yellow Submarine toy, made in Great Britain, fine, 5" x 2-1/4" x 2-3/4", and a Sheffield mini-alarm wind-up clock marked "West Germany," very good, 2-1/4" x 4" x 1-1/2", **$563 for set**.

Courtesy of Heritage Auctions

Ramp walking toy, circa 1934, punch-out set inspired by the components of the Blue Ribbon Waddle Book but featuring Mickey Mouse and Pluto, most text on the various pieces is in Japanese, pieces marked "Patent Syutsugansumi/Nakatani Gangu Seisaku/Sennichimae Osaka," rare, 8" x 10-1/2" x 16" l, **$1,500**.

Courtesy of Hakes Americana & Collectibles

Play set, 1975, Marvel Comics Group, Amsco set No. 9256, accompanied by stand-up figures Spider-Man, Captain America, Iron Man, Thor, Dr. Strange, Daredevil, 13-1/2" x 20" x 1" d, **$215**.

Courtesy of Hakes Americana & Collectibles

Ack-Ack Down A WWII Nazi Dive-Bomber, circa early 1940s, maker unknown, die-cut novelty game, contains intricately designed die-cut thin cardboard pieces that fit together to form, 11-3/4" w x 14" h table top display, top piece has silhouettes of three planes with text: "Down A Dornier, Junk A Junkers, Finish A Focke-Wulf," **$569**.

Courtesy of Hakes Americana & Collectibles

CHAPTER 13

How to Flip Your Toys

Picker Keith Moniz of Fairhaven, Massachusetts, is a seller of vintage items, but he's found profit and volume sales through vintage toys. Moniz's business is called Magoo's General Store, Inc. He is part of a new generation of sellers to entirely embrace online selling in favor of staffing and paying rent on a brick and mortar storefront. It makes sense: 21st century virtual traffic trumps the volume and cash flow seen on Main Street. Moniz holds sales on LiveAuctioneers and maintains inventory on eBay and 11 Main.com.

He's also among the first to sell items through Amazon.com, which made headlines in 2014 when it announced a major expansion in the collectibles realm. The site's estimated 144 million unique monthly visitors trump toy clearinghouse eBay nearly two to one. As of early 2015, Amazon does not attract the inventory or the collectors that drive big sales and most of Moniz's older inventory is sold elsewhere.

The variety of vintage toys to be found at toy shows is diverse and deep. A selection of vintage NASA space models are offered next to *Star Wars* action figures and contemporary vinyl figures, above. At left are lead and tin soldiers, a popular and highly sought-after corner of the antique toy hobby, which may be found at practically every large-scale collectibles show. A selection of Barclay soldiers were priced as low as $18 at a Brimfield Antiques Show. *Courtesy of Eric Bradley*

It's easy to see why online sites are competing to own a part of the collectible toy market. Because toys are small, they make the ideal inventory to pack and ship (a chief reason why so many toy shows dried up between 1995 and 2005). The pros and cons, however, must be considered before you plunge in, Moniz warns. "You're paying for their traffic," he said. "It's relatively easy to list on sites but the downside is that although it's your business, you don't have total control. They lure you with discounts but you have to run your business on their terms."

Selling online is way more difficult than it used to be, Moniz said. "It's all timing," he said. Among his tips:

- You'll have to abide by certain guidelines and meet certain metrics to garner the most exposure for your listings and to be eligible for discounts on fees. Amazon pushes for sellers to use their FBA program (Fulfillment by Amazon) because it a great revenue generator for them. If you're not sending your merchandise to their fulfillment centers, chances are slim that you will get the "Buy Box." That's Amazon's term for being featured on the center of the page while other sellers are relegated to a mention on the right side of the page.

- Visit sold listings of similar toys to see if lots of people are watching the auction. If so, the timing is probably right to post your piece. Condition is extremely important and will greatly influence what buyers are willing to pay for a vintage or collectible toy.

- The run up to Christmas is a hot time on eBay as buyers seek gifts and collectors find an excuse to splurge on a purchase.

A favorite online source is ProxiBid. The site is the go-to choice for rural auctioneers and mid-grade collections with individual items valued at less than $1,000 each. Online bid-

Picker's Tip

In September 2014, online auction juggernaut eBay added the following categories to match the increase in demand in new areas of toy collecting: Minifigure Parts & Accessories (LEGO); Magnetic Building Sets; Marble Runs; Storage, Mats & Play Tables; Cube, Twist Puzzles.

Auction houses group toys into one lot for a variety of reasons, but chiefly to increase final values. This group is comprised of a 17-inch German tin wind-up Ferris wheel by DC, together with a peacock and a clown on a scooter. It sold for **$2,750** in February 2014. *Courtesy of Leslie Hindman Auctioneers*

ding only takes place during the auction and competes against the floor bidders on site. Advance bid and proxy bids may be left on the site before the auction starts. The site hosts art, antiques and collectibles auctions as well as estates and personal property.

Auctions are the most effective means to help buyers find good toys and help sellers find fresh inventory. The trick is selecting which auction to attend. "If you're looking for bargains and looking for cheap toys then avoid a toy auction," Moniz advised, "because the collectors are there and they'll pay what it takes to get it. The best deals are found at regular estate auctions and the small amount of toys there that are oddballs in the auction."

If you aren't already familiar with the toy's rarity, don't buy broken toys or toys in rough condition. They may be cheap, but they will be much tougher to sell let alone deliver a profit.

"You can't buy junk toys. You're going to lose a lot of money," he said. "You've got to buy working toys." If you really want a toy and it's not in working order, be prepared to pay a hefty price for repair and/or parts. If you can fix them yourself, you have great advantage. Keep in mind, however, that buyers

Collectors are drawn to interactive toys. This Musical Jolly Chimp battery-operated toy by Daishin, Japan, has sold for as low as $20 to as much as $175 in mint condition with the original box. This example was offered during Michigan's Kalamazoo Circus Maximus Toy Show, held twice a year. *Courtesy of Jack Kelly*

expect sellers to disclose any repairs or parts that have been replaced.

WHERE TO BUY AND SELL

Today's buyers and sellers have access to more toys and customers than any time in history. All of the following are solid resources to help you buy and sell. Chief among these tips and techniques is that adding new and interesting toys to your collection takes one common denominator: Contacts. While you'll occasionally score a lucky snipe on eBay or be the only toy collector at a rural country auction, one of your best bets in adding great pieces is by letting lots of people know what you collect.

AUCTION HOUSES: A number of specialty toy auction houses exist all over the United States and Europe, but you can find great examples at nearly every auction house. Seek those with a solid reputation; a list can be found in the bibliography.

ADVERTISE: Place as many ads as your budget allows. Online, in print, on postcards, whatever it takes. I've seen well-respected business people don custom T-shirts proclaiming, "I Collect Tin Toys" and walk through huge flea markets. While not all of us have the nerve to become walking billboards, learn what you can from the approach: You'd be surprised what you'll find if people simply know what you're selling.

E-MAILS: Collect the email addresses of as many toy collectors and toy auction houses as possible. Share your want lists and items you wish to sell once every few months or so. Make sure you add dealer's e-mail addresses as well – you never know when your collector's eye could lead to a side business as a picker.

WEBSITE: Consider launching a collecting website. Free websites are available through WIX.com, Wordpress.com, or through your local internet service provider. A URL costs less than $10 to secure. Add a steady stream of photos and content and (working with your email list) you can quickly develop a following of buyers and sellers.

FACEBOOK and TWITTER: If you already have a small community around your area of interest, consider taking the lead and create a Facebook Fan Page. You can quickly generate a small army of collectors to like a page that delivers a fresh stream of interesting photos, facts, or observations of specialty toys. For instance, the Facebook Community devoted to "Gi Joe Toy Collectors" has more than 4,300 fans. The page for "Toy Collectors" has nearly 500 fans and regularly posts photos of new Chinese knockoffs collectors discover on their hunts.

As for Twitter, I find it a great source of breaking news on really important trends and new discoveries. Thanks to Twitter, I learned a rare copy of *Stadium Events* for the Nintendo Entertainment System sold for $35,100 on eBay within minutes of its sale.[24] Following important toy collectors such as Jordan Hembrough (@JordanHembrough); TBD Toys (@DanaFitkowski); Daniel Pickett (@AFInsider); Cool and Collected (@cool_collected); Toy Collector (@ToyCollectorApp) and Kevin Smith (@KevinSmith) will keep you in the loop on the latest releases and news.

GARAGE SALES and YARD SALES: Among the collectors I've talked to, buying toys directly from homes is often *the best* way to find amazing pieces and prices. It pays to get up early, and be there just as soon as the sale opens. Successful buyers are willing to show up the day before and politely ask the seller if they can look around. Tread lightly here; some don't like to be pestered during set up – even by collectors. And I always issue this plea: If you find a toy with a resale value worth several hundred dollars, please take the high road and offer the seller a fair value. Just because you're in the right place at the right time doesn't mean you have to be stingy.

ESTATE SALES: If a house is large enough to be managed by

---

24 On Jan. 15, 2015; Factory sealed 1987 Nintendo *NES Stadium Events* - VGA 85 NM+, eBay.

an estate company, you can be all but certain to find a few toys among the treasures. An excellent resource is EstateSales.net, a clearinghouse of sales held coast to coast. In my experience, estate companies often price their toys to leave resellers a bit of a resale profit margin – 20 to 30 percent – but this isn't always the case. Staff would rather spend time researching paintings, jewelry, and coins. Some estate companies will even allow you to sell your toys in a sale for a percentage of the price. Each company is different so it's best to get to know the owners and ask around if you're curious.

SWAP MEETS and FLEA MARKETS: Found all over world, swap meets and flea markets are an ideal source of great toys, Hot Wheels and Matchbox cars, and vintage video games. The same rules apply here as in garage sales: Go early, preferably as soon as the place opens. Haggle and don't be afraid to politely offer a ridiculously low price. It's the seller's responsibility to know the value of their inventory; you can land a good deal without being rude. You should take a moment to chat up the seller to learn more about what you collect. Share what you know. What's the point of a day of bargain hunting if you don't learn something new, too?

NEWSPAPER CLASSIFIED ADS: Despite what you've read online, daily newspapers are not dead and they are read by families who happen to have lots of toys, especially from the 1950s and 1960s. In my experience, newspaper subscribers may not be placing many classified ads, but they are reading them. Ads in community newspapers seeking to buy toys nearly always generate calls.

SMALL TOY SHOWS: Even toy shows packed with action figures and Hot Wheels cars hold tin toy rarities. I recently found a circa 1950s Greyhound Bus tin friction toy made by Storm of Japan at a monthly toy show stocked with mainly contemporary plastic collectibles. The toy regularly sells for twice the purchase price online. Every large metropolitan area has a toy show and an excellent source for upcoming events is the Show Calendar published in *Antique Trader Magazine* in print and online at antiquetrader.com/showcalendar. Small shows will charge you as little as $25 a space to $75 for a space and a 6-foot table or as much as $250 a 10 x 10 space if the show is heavily advertised to advanced collectors.

CRAIGSLIST: Searchcraigslist.org is a portal to every community touched by the classified ad site Craigslist.org. It is a favorite haunt of vintage video game collectors. Searches conducted over a full quarter period in 2014 show as many as 500 different ads for tin toys and many more for vintage video games. Remember: just because you found it online, doesn't mean the seller is willing to work a long-distance transaction.

ONLINE AUCTIONS: Despite thousands of tin toys listed at any one time, eBay is still a wonderful source of great examples. Don't be shy in asking the seller for additional images of a toy and make sure you understand the word "rare" is often only used just to catch your attention.

PUBLICATIONS: *Antique Toy World* and *Classic Toy Trains Magazine* are reliable sources of serious collector contact networking as well as cutting edge research into makers and new discoveries. Back issues are fascinating resources. Speaking of which, don't dismiss picking up back issues of defunct magazines such as *Model and Toy Collector*, *Marx Toy Collector*, *Toy Shop*, and *Barbie Bazaar* to glean knowledge on vintage toys. Even copies of the obscure *Toy World and Bicycle World* (Chilton Co.), a retailer publication popular in the 1930s, give crisp images and design details on quality toys sold in stores at the time. You can find these and more with a quick internet search, but especially on eBay.

SHOPGOODWILL.COM: As the site states, this is "Goodwill's online auction site offering a wide array of antiques, collectibles, books, and much more – culled from Goodwill's vast inventory." A recent search turned up more than 4,500 unique listings of toys, dolls and games, ranging from a vintage 1970s Roto Robot for $400 to a LEGO Simpson's House (set #71006) for $148. Payment must be made within seven days of the auction's close and select Goodwills now accept PayPal. The trick with this site is to pay attention to where the item is located simply to monitor shipping rates. The software isn't as slick as eBay's, but by shopping your local Goodwill, you can save on shipping costs by picking up the item after the auction. Some locations – such as the Goodwill of Orange County – charge a "handling fee" ranging from $2 to as much as $5 regardless of delivery method including pickup.

Resources

BIBLIOGRAPHY

Bellomo, Mark. *The Ultimate Guide to Vintage Star Wars Action Figures 1977-1985*. Iola. Krause Publications, 2014.

Bellomo, Mark. *Toys & Prices*, 19th Edition. Iola: Krause Publications, 2013.

Bradley, Eric. *Antique Trader Antiques & Collectibles 2015 Price Guide*. Iola: Krause Publications, 2014.

Bruce, Scott. *Cereal Boxes and Prizes: 1960s*. Cambridge, Mass.: Flake World Publishing, 1998.

Daiken, Leslie. *Children's Toys Throughout the Ages*. London: Spring Books, 1965.

Folley Dan. *Toys Through The Ages*. Philadelphia: Chilton Books, 1962.

Foulke, Jan. *Jan Foulke's Guide to Dolls*. Braintree, Mass.: Bangzoom Publishers, 2006.

Gardiner, Gordon and Morris Alistair. *Metal Toys*. London: Salamander Books, 1984.

Herman, Sarah. *A Million Little Bricks*. New York: Skyhorse, 2012.

Kendrick, Kathleen, Liebhold, Peter. *Smithsonian Treasures of American History*. New York: Harper Collins, 2006.

Ketchum, William. *Toys and Games*. United States: Smithsonian Institution, 1981.

Khayos, Tom. "Toy Grading and Why it's Not Worth Your Time or Money." Raging Nerdgasm. Jan. 15, 2012. Web. Sept. 21, 2014.

Lazar, Allan, Karlan, Dan, Salter, Jeremy. *The 101 Most Influential People Who Never Lived*. New York: Harper, 2006.

Lipkowitz, Daniel. *The Lego Book*. New York: DK, 2009.

Newnum, Donna and Suiters, Loretta. *Schroeder's Collectible Toys Antique to Modern Price Guide*. Kentucky: Schroeder, 2008.

Opie, James. *20th Century Toys*. New Jersey: Studio Editions, 1990.

Parr, Martin. *Parr World: Objects*. New York: Chris Boot Ltd. 2008.

Pearsall, Ronald. *A Connoisseur's Guide to Antique Toys*. New York: Todri Productions, 1999.

Pressland, David. *The Art of the Tin Toy*. New York: Crown Publishers, 1976.

Robinson, Matthew, Karp, Jensen. *Just Can't Get Enough.* New York: Abrams Image, 2007.

Sansweet, Stephen and Ling, Josh. *Star Wars the Action Figure Archive.* Hong Kong: Chronicle Books, 1999.

Sansweet, Stephen. *Star Wars: From Concept to Screen to Collectible.* China: Chronicle Books, 1992.

Walsh, Tim. *The Playmakers.* Sarasota, Fla.: Keys Publishing, 2004.

Ward, Arthur. *Classic Toys of the 1960s and 1970s.* Ramsbury, Marlborough, England: Crowood Press, 2008.

Young, Mark, Duin, Steve, Richardson Mike. *Blast Off.* Milwaukie, Ore.: Dark Horse Books, 2012.

Zarnock, Michael. *Hot Wheels Variations, 2000-2013: Identification and Price Guide.* Iola, Wis.: Krause Publications, 2014.

"DiCaprio Follows the Colonel's Lead." Web log post. Whopper's Bunker. N.p., 27 Mar. 2006. Web. 26 Nov. 2014. <http://genthar.blogspot.com/>.

AUCTIONEERS · AUCTION HOUSES · RETAILERS

Bertoia Auctions

2141 DeMarco Drive; Vineland, NJ 08360

856-692-1881; fax: 856-692-8697

toys@BertoiaAuctions.com; bertoiaauctions.com

Bonhams Auctioneers

220 San Bruno Ave.; San Francisco, CA 94103

(415) 861-7500; fax: (415) 861 8951

info.us@bonhams.com; bonhams.com

GameGavel.com

A host to more than one million vintage video game auctions and unique gaming community and the RetroGamingRoundup.com podcast.

Game Over Videogames*

2136 Rutland Dr, Suite A; Austin, TX 78758

512-459-GAME (4263); info@gameovervideogames.com

Online store: sales@gameovervideogames.com

gameovervideogames.com

*10 retail locations around the country

Heritage Auctions

3500 Maple Ave.; Dallas, TX 75219.3941

877-437-4824; Bid@ha.com; ha.com

James D. Julia, Inc.

203 Skowhegan Rd.; Fairfield, ME 04937

800-565-9298; info@jamesdjulia.com; jamesdjulia.com

JMW Auction Gallery

612 Washington Ave.; Kingston, NY 12401

845-339-4133; jay@jmwauction.com; jmwauction.com

Magoo's General Store, Inc.

Keith M. Moniz

70 Elm Street; Fairhaven, MA 02719-6906

(774) 582-3000; fax: 508-996-6694

magoosinc@gmail.com

stores.ebay.com/Magoos-General-Store-Inc

Liveauctioneers.com/Magoos-General-Store

Morphy Auctions

2000 N. Reading Rd.; Denver, PA 17517

717-335-3435; morphy@morphyauctions.com;

morphyauctions.com

Paige Auction

6429 SW Macadam Ave.; Portland, OR 97239

503-477-6307; info@paigeauction.com; paigeauction.com

Philip Weiss Auctions

74 Merrick Road; Lynbrook, NY 11563

(516) 594-0731; Fax: (516) 594-9414; info@weissauctions.com;

weissauctions.com

Profiles in History

26662 Agoura Road; Calabasas, CA 91302

(310) 859-7701; Fax: (310) 859-3842;

info@profilesinhistory.com; profilesinhistory.com

Rich Penn Auctions

P.O. Box 1355; Waterloo, IA 50704

319-291-6688; info@richpennauctions.com; richpennauctions.com

RSL Auction Co.

P.O. Box 635; Oldwick, NJ 08858

908-823-4049; cell: 917-991-7352; fax: 908-823-4519;

leonweiss@me.com; rslauctions.com

Skinner Auctioneers & Appraisers of Objects of Value

skinnerinc.com; info@skinnerinc.com

Skinner Boston

63 Park Plaza; Boston, MA 02116

617-350-5400

Skinner Marlborough

274 Cedar Hill St.; Marlborough, MA 01752

508-970-3000

Skinner Miami

2332 Galiano St., 2nd Floor; Coral Gables, FL 33134

305-503-4423

Stout Auctions of Premier Model Trains

529 SR 28 East; Williamsport, IN 47993

765-764-6901; fax: 765-764-1516

info@stoutauctions.com; stoutauctions.com

Theriault's Antique Doll Auctions

PO Box 151; Annapolis, MD 21404

800-638-0422; fax: 410-224-2515; theriaults.com

Thomaston Place Auction Galleries

PO Box 300; Thomaston, Maine 04861

207-354-8141; Fax: 207-354-9523; auction@kajav.com;
thomastonauction.com

Toybase 10

4028 Northwest 10th St.; Oklahoma City, OK 73107

405-601-4480; baseinvade@aol.com

ToyTent.com - Karen Dozier

P.O. Box 412; Ponderay, ID 83852

kdozier@toytent.com

William Morford Investment Grade Collectibles at Auction

RD #2 Cobb Hill Road; Cazenovia, NY 13035

(315) 662-7625; fax: (315) 662-3570; morf2bid@aol.com;
morfauction.com

DEALERS/RESELLERS

Kyle O'Neil

Gunsmith – a seller of loose *Star Wars* weapons
and accessories from 2000-2012.

Lewisville, Texas; another.todia@gmail.com

Scott Walker

Marvel Legends Series Action Figures

Allen, Texas; mswalker528@yahoo.com

XCES studios LLC

3224 US Hwy 41 W Suite 179; Marquette, MI 49855

Design studio for custom environments for

1/6 scale action figures

906-869-4081; xcesstudios.com; Facebook: XCES studios LLC

ONLINE AUCTION PROVIDERS

eBay.com; LiveAuctioneers.com; Proxibid.com; iCollector.com; the-saleroom.com

PUBLICATIONS

Antique Toy World Magazine

Since 1970, the world's leading monthly magazine published for the toy collecting community. Published and edited in the United States by Dale Kelley.

PO Box 34509; Chicago, IL 60634

773-725-0633; fax 773-725-3449; antiquetoyworld.com

Old Toy Soldier Magazine

Since 1976, offering articles and regular features on all aspects of collecting toy soldiers and figures.

Published quarterly; oldtoysoldier.com

RETRO Magazine

ReadRetro.com

Offering six collectible issues a year printed on high-quality stock, RETRO in-depth knowledge and insight into the games market from the last 30+ years.

Toy Soldier Collector Magazine

toysoldiercollector.com

Print and online magazine for all collectors, includes figures and set reviews for new, metal and plastic in every issue.

Toy Collector Magazine

Toyzine.com

Offers online retailing opportunities; For Sale and Wanted classifieds, ecommerce websites; an e-magazine; e-newsletters; and an appraisal and valuation service.

COLLECTOR'S SITES

Alphadrome; danefield.com

Leading web site for collectors of tin toy robots and vintage space toys from the 1930s to the present.

Cool and Collected; coolandcollected.com

Devoted to vintage toys, new releases, pop culture, movie memorabilia and collectibles.

ToyMania.com

Expansive collectors' focus with information on action figures, old and new. Features archives, up-to-date news, previews, chat room, shopping and links on vintage toys, fast food premiums and more.

WishbookWeb.com

Pre-eminent catalog preservation site of holiday toys. This is a free site featuring a collector's assemblage of hard-to-find catalogs. Each is scanned in high resolution, offering collectors a wonderful resource to learn how toys were marketed and described by original manufacturers.

Sideshow Collectors Forums

Up to the minute discussions on the latest toys, events and custom innovations.
Sideshowcollectors.com/forums/content

One Sixth Republic

Facebook Community where collectors can unwind, read reviews and chat with each other about their favorite collectibles. Dedicated to 1/6 collectibles (Hot Toys, Sideshow, Enterbay, Medicom, etc) but welcome discussion of any collectible.
Facebook.com/OneSixthRepublic

CLUBS

Antique Toy Collectors of America

Non-profit 501(c)(3) organization designed to preserve the history of toys, to educate its membership and the public as to the history and preservation of toys, and to share fellowship and friendship through the common bond of owning toys and sharing information about toys. Members must own a minimum of five antique toys.

atca-club.org

United Federation of Doll Clubs

Extensive association of doll clubs, doll history and more.

10900 N. Pomona Avenue; Kansas City, MO 64153

816-891-7040; fax: 816-891-8360; ufdc.org

Boston Area Toy Collectors Club

Comprised of a diverse membership of collectors ranging from die-cast vehicles to urban vinyl. Club meets monthly and hosts presentations in addition to the annual National Collectible Toy Event, held each September.

sjlanzilla@yahoo.com; bostontoyclub.com

Cracker Jack Collectors Association

CJCA is dedicated to the collecting of Cracker Jack prizes and related items; members of all ages.

crackerjackcollectors.com

Train Collectors Association

Founded in 1954, this worldwide organization is approaching 30,000 members, with many local divisions and chapters.

PO Box 248; Strasburg, PA 17579-0248

300 Paradise Lane; Ronks, PA 17572

717-687-8623; fax: 717-687-0742; tca-office@traincollectors.org; traincollectors.org

EVENTS

Antique City Fun Fair - every April

LeHigh University Fieldhouse

123 Goodman Drive; Bethlehem, PA

Show office: 109 Delmar Avenue; Linwood, NJ 08221

info@antiquecityshow.com; antiquecityshow.com

Brimfield Antiques Shows

Three times a year: May, July, September

Brimfield, MA 01010

Visit Hertan's Antique Show, J&J Promotions, Sturtevants North, Collins Apple Barn, New England Motel, Heart-O-The Mart, and May's Antique Market.

Kalamazoo Circus Maximus Toy Show

Kalamazoo County Expo Center

2900 Lake Street; Kalamazoo, MI 49048

Fall Show: Always on the Friday and Saturday after Thanksgiving; Spring Show: Always on the 3rd Friday and Saturday in May

uniqueeventsshows.com

North Dallas Toy Show

Valley View Center Mall

13331 Preston Rd; Dallas, TX 75240

NorthDallasToyShow@gmail.com; http://northdallastoyshow. wix.com/toys; facebook.com/northdallastoyshow

First Saturday of every month; show promoter Doug Kale

Index

About the Author

Eric Bradley is the author of the critically-acclaimed *Mantiques: A Manly Guide to Cool Stuff*, *Picker's Pocket Guide: Signs* and the editor of the annual *Antique Trader Antiques & Collectibles Price Guide*.

A former editor of *Antique Trader* magazine and an award-winning investigative journalist with a degree in economics, he has appeared in *The Wall Street Journal*, *GQ*, *Four Seasons Magazine*, *Bottom Line/Personal* and *The Detroit News*, among others.

He is a public relations associate at Heritage Auctions, HA.com, the world's largest collectibles auctioneer, and lives near Dallas with his wife and three children.